QUIVER RIVER

David Carkeet

A Laura Geringer Book

An Imprint of HarperCollins*Publishers*

Quiver River
Copyright © 1991 by David Carkeet
All rights reserved. No part of this book may be used or reproduced in any
manner whatsoever without written permission except in the case of brief
quotations embodied in critical articles and reviews. Printed in the United States
of America. For information address HarperCollins Children's Books, a division
of HarperCollins Publishers, 10 East 53rd Street, New York, NY 10022.
Typography by Christine Hoffman
1 2 3 4 5 6 7 8 9 10
First Edition

Library of Congress Cataloging-in-Publication Data
Carkeet, David.
  Quiver River / by David Carkeet.
    p.   cm.
  "A Laura Geringer book."
  Summary: Teenage Ricky describes his experiences working a summer
job at a lake resort.
  ISBN 0-06-022453-3. — ISBN 0-06-022454-1 (lib. bdg.)
  [1. Humorous stories.]   I. Title.
PZ7.C21472Qu   1991   90-24095
[Fic]—dc20   CIP
                                                                AC

To Cory, Jessica, Brian, Brent, and Tristan

One

Look at these hands. Look at them. They can do anything.

Look at the sure grasp, the delicate touch. A surgeon's hands.

Look at their athletic power. A quarterback's hands.

Look at the curve of the fingers, their long reach. A pianist's hands.

The thing is, I clean toilets.

Don't give up on me. It's not my long-term career or anything. It's just a summer job at this lake resort in the mountains, thirty miles up the highway from my home in Ragtown. Quiver Lake, it's called. I have a great view when I step outside for fresh air, and I do a lot of that, believe me. Through the pine trees I can see the lake, with babes on the beach. I can see boats on the water, with babes in them. Far across the lake I can see big blocks of granite, with babes sunbathing on them.

Nate says I have babes on the brain. He's my best friend, and he's got a job here too. He works in general maintenance around the campground. Me, I work in specific maintenance.

The thing is, cleaning toilets doesn't put you in a classy position for romance. I clump around in my work clothes (long-sleeved brown shirt, jeans, boots), and I push this cart with a big barrel on it and brooms and mops sticking out of it. When I pass by the girls in their swimming suits, I feel like I disappear right before their eyes. To make things worse, most of them are in college. Nate and I will be seniors at Ragtown High this fall. If you *really* want to disappear, tell a college girl you're in high school. You'll go *poof,* just like magic.

Here's the layout. Quiver Lake is big, first of all, impossible for most people to swim across, especially at this elevation, where you get winded fast. Three of its four sides are steep—basically mountains—with blocks of granite at the base of them, near the water's edge. On the side where we work it's flat, with a beach and a piney, shady area right behind it for picnicking. Then the toilets—my domain. There are seven of them, wooden buildings spread along the edge of the picnic area. Beyond the toilets is the campground, and beyond this are the summer rental cabins. Nate and I are staying in one of those.

Rodney's up here too. He's my brother. He just finished his first year of college, where he's busy acquiring knowledge in order to tell everyone about it at the earliest opportunity. One of his professors, a woman, chose him and some other students for this special summer course on Miwok Indian life in the Sierras. She's got them living up the river on the other side of the lake in these bark huts that they've built. They're having this total experience. Rodney talks about it constantly. He drives me nuts.

Here's my routine. At eight A.M. I report to work. (This sounds impressive. All it really means is I walk from our cabin to the toolshed near the picnic tables.) At eight fifteen I report to my first assignment (Toilet Number One). I establish that the area is secure. (This means I call into the women's john, "All clear?") Then I commence operations. (Figure it out.) It takes about an hour to do a complete toilet, women's and men's sides. When I'm done I make my way to Toilet Number Two, zigzagging through the picnic area with my cart to pick up trash on the way. I do four toilets in the morning, take a half hour for lunch, and do three toilets in the afternoon. That's my day. That's it.

I always take an afternoon break at the outdoor theater in the picnic area. I grab a soda from the machine there and sprawl out on one of the long log benches. The theater is where the local forest ranger gives a program one night a week, and the other nights they show movies. Nate and I already saw this week's movie—*Star Trek IV*, where they travel back to our time for humpback whales. It was a good movie to see outdoors, because now and then I'd look up at the treetops, and it didn't seem unreasonable that a spaceship could suddenly drop into my life.

Which is actually a funny feeling I have about this whole summer: that something—not a spaceship, but *something*—is going to drop into my life.

TWO

There's another thing I do every day that gives me comfort in my lowly occupation. As I work my way through the picnic grounds from one toilet to the next, I look through the trees and search out a certain orange buoy on the lake. When I spot it, it makes me smile every time.

Here's why: In the summer the county newspaper, the *Ragtown Daily*, runs a big treasure hunt to celebrate the California Gold Rush. The treasure that everyone looks for is two thousand dollars. Starting in June, clues appear every Friday in the paper. Who writes them is a big mystery, almost as big a mystery as where the treasure is. Eventually someone figures out the clues and finds the hiding place. Last year that someone was Nate and me, with Rodney coming in a dirty second. When Nate and I discovered the hiding place, we discovered something else as well, something almost as good as the treasure itself: The winner gets to pick next year's hiding place and write the clues for the hunt.

We had the whole year to think about it. We considered places all over the county. When we got our summer jobs, we decided to hide the treasure somewhere near Quiver Lake, so we could keep an eye on the progress of the hunt. Then we decided to put it *in* the lake. Nate's dad is pretty handy, and he made a waterproof metal box for us. We put the document in it that entitles the finder to go to the *Daily* office and claim the two thousand bucks, and we sealed it up good. Then, early one morning in May, Nate and I paddled a rowboat out to the orange buoy. It's anchored to the lake bottom by a long cable, and we hooked the box to the cable so that it could slide down it. We lowered it by wire about ten feet and tied the wire to the cable just below the surface.

It's a terrific hiding place. No one's going to find it by accident, which is the worst possible thing that can happen. You can't see the box from the surface. You can't even see the wire unless you're looking for it. No swimmers are going to come across it, because swimming is allowed only along the shore, on account of the boat traffic. But once someone solves the clues, they'll be able to take a boat out there and pull that wire and land the treasure just like hauling in a rainbow trout.

As far as I was concerned, there was just one disadvantage to the place we picked: Rodney. He was the last person in the world I wanted to find the treasure. When we "buried" it in the lake, I figured Rodney would be at Stanford all summer, since he'd said he was going to take a summer class. But then he announced the class would be up here, which meant he'd be living practically on top of the money. There was another side to it though—the fun of listening to him wallow in ignorance as he wondered out loud where it might be hidden. He had no idea Nate and I were the authors of the clues. He even thought we were looking for the treasure ourselves.

It had been a tough day, toiletwise, and I was looking forward to getting back to the cabin. I rolled my cart from Toilet Number Seven back to the toolshed. I padlocked the door and walked through the campground, grinning like a maniac because it was Friday. My work week was over, and I had the Friday-night dance to look forward to. The possibilities were endless.

When I opened the back door to the cabin, I heard Nate's voice from the living room. I stopped in the laundry room, where the door opened, and listened. It was silent. Who had he been talking to? A girl? Maybe there were *two* girls. Nate was enough of a charmer for this to be possible. He could have met them while he was working and invited them here for dinner. I tiptoed to the bathroom to wash the Comet cleanser smell off my hands. I checked myself in the mirror (not bad!) and combed my hair. Then I messed it up to make it look like I hadn't just combed it. I gave my face a final check. Okay. Go get 'em.

Nate was sitting all by himself in the living room. He wasn't watching TV, the radio wasn't on, and there was no phone in there he could have been using. He was just sitting there. It was like he had been talking to Jeannie in the old TV show, and she had blinked her eyes and disappeared when she heard me coming.

"Hi, Ricky," he said.

"What are you doing?" I said.

"Nothing."

"Who were you talking to?"

"Norman the Foreman."

This was our boss, a guy in his forties that Nate worked with almost every day. I looked around the room and out the windows onto the front porch. "Where is he?" I asked.

"I don't know." Nate stretched and yawned.

"Was he here?"

"No. I was just saying everything I wanted to say to him all day. I can't really do it to his face—not if I want to keep my job." Nate couldn't stand Norman. "Tell me, Ricky, why is Norman so bald? Is it because he pounded his taco too much when he was our age?"

"No," I said as I sat down on the couch. "It's because he didn't pound it enough."

Nate laughed.

"I thought you had some babes in here," I said.

"Geez, don't you ever think of anything else?"

I put my feet up on the coffee table, boots and all. "I guess not. Except for food. What's for dinner?"

"Isn't it your turn?"

"Nope. Last night nobody cooked, and I cooked the night before that. Hot dogs, remember?"

Nate moaned. He got up and headed into the kitchen. "I hate this. It's the worst part."

"Yeah. My mom was right."

"Agh!" he yelled. "Don't ever say that."

I leaned forward and began to untie my boots, thinking how Mom wouldn't like the way I was using the edge of the coffee table to support them. When I got the job, she immediately opposed the idea of me living up here. She even offered me the use of her car for the thirty-mile commute from Ragtown to Quiver Lake. But I really wanted to live here for the summer, and Dad and I eventually wore her down. He liked the idea of me getting out on my own.

"What are you gonna make?" I yelled toward the kitchen.

"Hot dogs."

I laughed. "Real original. If my mom calls, it was chef salad."

"Okay. What about last night?"

"Zucchini casserole."

"Geez. You better tell her. I'd start laughing."

One of the things that had worried Mom was that I wouldn't eat right. She made me promise over and over that I would. Nate and I started off strong, but things deteriorated pretty fast. We'd begun inventing fictitious meals, and we'd report on these to Mom. It was hard to keep track of them, though—almost as hard as cooking the stupid things.

"I got a *Daily*," Nate said over the sound of a banging pot. "It's on the coffee table. You see anybody snooping around the buoy?"

"No. We're safe so far." On top of the pile of books and magazines on the table was the *Ragtown Daily*. I looked at the clue in the upper-right-hand corner.

Two thousand, three thousand,
four thousand, five.
What are these numbers? Man alive!

Is it people, is it stars, is it chickens or eggs?
Or is it those things at the ends of your legs?

The last line was the key. It was supposed to make you think of feet—in the sense of elevation, because Quiver Lake was at five thousand feet above sea level.

This was our third clue of the summer. Nate had written it (we took turns), and I was nervous about it. When he showed it to me early in the week, I told him it gave away too much. We argued about it a little. He said readers would imagine human feet walking around, not elevation-type feet. I didn't agree at first, then I did, then I didn't again. It was hard to know how people would think.

Nate crossed the living room and began to sort through the cassette tapes. They belonged to the owner of the cabin, who lived here in the winter, and so far we'd been disappointed. The guy's musical tastes didn't make any sense at all. "So," Nate said, "how's the clue look in print?"

I sighed. "As poetry, forget it. 'Eggs' is forced. You can tell that the author is stuck for a rhyme for 'legs,' and 'eggs' is the best he can do, but then to make 'eggs' look good he hauls in 'chickens,' and you wonder what he's going to haul in next."

Nate was staring at me, his mouth stuck half open. I knew the look. It meant he couldn't believe how I was going on and on. Nate and I knew each other pretty well.

"It's good," I concluded quickly. "Especially the last line."

"'Or is it those things at the ends of your legs?'" Nate called out, sort of dramatically.

I laughed. "You got it memorized? You're really in love with it, aren't you?"

"Yeah," Nate said as he pawed through the cassettes. "I think it's a kick to write something for the newspaper and have thousands of people scratching their heads over it. Hey! Here's a Billy Joel. The owner's not a *complete* idiot." He turned on the cassette player and put the tape in. It was a good sound, and it filled the cabin. "You'll have to get to work on next week's clue, Ricky. Try to make it build on mine—the elevation idea."

"What if it doesn't need any building on? What if people are swarming all over the lake tomorrow?"

"Nah," said Nate. "People aren't that smart. No sweat."

There was a loud knock at the back door. Girls, I thought. Two of them. (I always thought of two. I didn't want one to come between Nate and me.) Lost and asking for directions. Or, better yet, the campground office had booked them into our cabin by mistake, and they'd have to spend the summer here. Beautiful girls. Good cooks, too.

I heard Nate open the back door. Then I heard someone say, "Greetings." My dream girls sounded an awful lot like Rodney.

"Greetings, brother," he said as he strolled into the kitchen. He came to a stop in front of the stove and sniffed.

"Want to stay for dinner?" Nate said to him.

"Ah," Rodney said. "A tempting offer, but no. I'm here to use the facilities." He held up a towel he'd brought with him.

"Right," I said. "Help yourself." Rodney used our shower two or three times a week. He could take only so much of the authentic Miwok Indian life. I wondered if his professor knew about it.

"I've taken the liberty of bringing some laundry as well." He produced a white cotton bag. "May I?"

"Sure," said Nate. "But don't start it until you're done with your shower. The water pressure's weak here."

"Ah," Rodney said. This "Ah" was something he had brought back from college. He used it whenever he understood something, no matter how trivial it was. You could say, "Rodney, you just stepped in something the dog left behind," and he would say

"Ah" as if you had explained the origin of the universe.

As I watched Rodney walk to the stairs, I wished Nate hadn't warned him about the water pressure. But that was typical of Nate—being nice to someone who was never nice back. Nate once told me he found Rodney "interesting." I just laughed. How "interesting" can a pain in the ass be?

Rodney paused at the foot of the stairs, listening.

"Something wrong?" I said. I wanted him to be gone.

He tilted his head slightly. He had a distant, intellectual look on his face. "That song," he said.

"It's Billy Joel." I looked at him. "It's called 'This Night.'"

"No it's not," Rodney said. "The melody is from Beethoven's 'Pathétique' Sonata. There. That part right there."

This bugged me. I always thought Billy Joel was pretty decent. "What are you saying? He stole it?"

"Not at all. He simply used it. The best composers do it all the time." Rodney turned to Nate, as if not wanting to waste his learning on me, a mere brother. "Beethoven used many common folk melodies himself. They all do it." He waited, then sang the stretch of music when it came up again, conducting it at the same time with his long skinny index finger. I really wished Nate hadn't told him about the water pressure.

Rodney was about to go upstairs when his eye fell on the newspaper. "Ah. Today's clue. What do you think?"

Nate and I shrugged and looked dumb. Nate had a way of looking innocent when he was up to something. His black hair would fall across his forehead into his eyes a little. That was the way he looked now.

"Keeping your ideas to yourselves, eh?" Rodney said. "All right. Be that way. I'm more generous. I'll tell you what I think. The things at the ends of your legs are feet, which can only mean elevation. The clue tells us the treasure is somewhere in the county at five thousand feet above sea level. Quiver Lake is at five thousand feet, so the treasure could be right around here. I'm surprised the clues got so helpful so fast. It usually takes longer to narrow down the area. It looks like a real blunder to me. Well, I'm going to go take a nice hot shower now."

Rodney trotted up the stairs. I looked at Nate. He did a funny thing to punish himself for writing such a failure of a clue. He made his hands slap his face fast, over and over, and he whipped his head back and forth with each blow, like a guy who was really taking a beating.

Three

After his shower, Rodney started his laundry and took off, leaving me with complex instructions about what to put in the dryer and what not to put in the dryer, which I instantly forgot.

Nate and I hung around the cabin until nine o'clock and then left for the dance. We wound our way through the campground. There was another way to get to the parking lot where the dances were held, but I liked the campground route. Everything was so out in the open, as if the rules for living had been changed and all the walls were torn down. You could hear morsels from everyone's life. "Hey, Mary, where's the toothpaste?" "You kids leave that fire alone." That sort of thing. Nothing exciting, but it was fun to eavesdrop.

Nate and I didn't talk. We were nervous, I guess. I always felt like someone had stabbed me in the stomach when a dance was coming up. I'd look forward to them all day, then panic when the time arrived. I said a few things as we walked, but Nate didn't respond much. He got real intense on Friday nights.

In the distance a group of guys on the beach were making their way to the dance. I could hear them shouting and fooling around, but it was too dark to see them. Now and then I heard a splash as they threw stuff into the lake. They started chanting, "Par-*dee*, par-*dee*."

When we got to the parking lot, we joined some friends of ours from Ragtown and checked out the situation. One of the guys was Gary, a pretty good friend who was easy to be with. He was funny, but you never knew if he meant to be. When we first got there, he kept asking me to smell him. He worked at the Ragtown dump, moving piles of garbage around with a little tractor, and he was afraid he'd brought the smell with him. I was going to tease him, but I saw he was really worried, so I just said I'd never known him to smell so good.

We stood together and watched the action. This mainly involved finding the most beautiful girls and making jokes about their partners. Nate was scoping everyone out, his eyes kind of narrow and burning.

Rodney suddenly appeared at my side. I was surprised to see him. He hadn't come to the first two dances of the summer, and he hadn't said a word about planning to come tonight. I was even more surprised to see that he had an actual human female person with him.

"You're probably wondering why I turned down your offer of dinner," he said.

"Not really," I said. The girl and I glanced at each other. I wondered if Rodney was going to introduce us. She wore glasses and was okay-looking. Not great-looking. Just okay-looking.

"Our class had a big meal," Rodney said. "That's why."

"Oh?"

"An authentic Miwok dinner. Acorn bread. Pine nuts. Roasted mariposa lily bulbs."

"Mm-hmm."

"Some grass seed. A squirrel."

"A squirrel?"

"Grasshoppers—"

"You're kidding."

"No, I'm not. And yellow jacket larvae."

I tried to imagine this. Then I tried not to. The girl said, "You were a real good eater, Rodney."

"Oh, but you were too, Maggie," Rodney said.

"You didn't just eat. You tasted it. Some of the others ate, but they breathed through their mouths so they wouldn't have to taste it so much. I saw them."

"For sheer quantity you were outstanding," she said.

Rodney got a proud, goofy smile on his face. Then he looked at me and said, "Ricky, this is Maggie. Maggie, this is my brother, Ricky."

"Ah," she said—just like Rodney.

I said hi.

"Maggie's a sophomore at Stanford," Rodney said. "She's a complete American Indian nut."

She smiled. "I'm most interested in their initiation rites."

"Really?" I said, trying to be polite. I looked at the dancers. They were going at it to a Rolling Stones song.

Maggie leaned toward me, grabbing my attention. "What is a man in Indian culture? What is a woman? Questions like those interest me."

This kind of talk seemed wildly out of place here. I looked to my other side. Nate and Gary were listening. They were watching Maggie with totally blank faces.

"In so-called primitive cultures," Maggie went on, "you've got clear-cut initiation rites—ceremonies that turn boys into men and girls into women. They can be very painful. Sometimes they're deprived of food and water for days, or they're beaten, or buried up to their necks. Sometimes they get cut up. A favorite area of cutting is the genitalia. All sorts of things happen there."

I nodded and took another look at Nate and Gary. They were listening, but they looked stupid-faced, like two guys who'd been watching TV all day.

"Miwoks are interesting. In their female initiation ceremony, a girl had to lie in a trench for four days while men danced around her. The men's faces were streaked with red paint."

Rodney chimed in, "To symbolize the blood of the first menstrual period." I heard a giggle from Gary.

"Exactly," Maggie said to Rodney.

"Is that how long a period lasts?" Nate asked. "Four days?" Rodney threw Nate a sharp look. He must have heard Gary's giggle and thought Nate was making fun of Maggie. But the question was sincere. I could tell. Nate wasn't sporting his innocent look with his hair across his forehead.

Maggie was a little slow to respond. Since she was the only one in the group who could speak from experience, we had to wait. "In terms of actual flow," she said, "four days is close. That just might explain why the ceremony lasts four days. It's a nice theory." She gave Nate an approving look. I thought it was a good time to introduce her to him and Gary, so I did.

Gary, following Nate's example, asked a serious question instead of giggling. "Did Miwok boys go through an initiation ceremony?"

Maggie responded with such excitement that Gary flinched a little. "I'm devoting my whole summer to that very question," she said. "There are legends that refer to an initiation for a few Miwok males, but no one has figured out what the rite involved. I'm interviewing the few Miwoks living in the county to see what they know, but so far I've had no luck. If they know anything, they're keeping silent about it for some reason. It's a mystery."

Gary mumbled something that made Nate laugh. I could see that Nate felt he should include us, and he spoke up. "Gary says maybe the boy's initiation rite was to lie in the trench with the girl for the four days."

I laughed. Rodney threw Nate a cold look. Maggie seemed to give the idea serious thought. She said in a crisp way, "I doubt it. My Miwok informants would have told me. I've urged them to be quite frank about sexual matters."

"Maggie's always frank about sexual matters," Rodney said. From anyone else this would have been a joke or a come-on. From Rodney it was a straight fact, like saying a beetle has a thorax.

"Good Thing" by the Fine Young Cannibals suddenly blasted over the loudspeakers, and Maggie said, "This has been fun. Now I'm ready for fun of a different kind." She reached out for Rodney and sort of dragged him to the dance floor, where they went at it. Neither of them had a clue about how to dance.

"Wow," said Gary, summing up his impression of Maggie, Maggie plus Rodney, their dancing—pretty much everything. Nate and I said "Yeah" in general agreement. Then I asked Gary how things were in Ragtown. I hadn't been there in three weeks.

"Same old boring place," Gary said. "The only excitement is the new clue in tonight's *Daily.*"

Nate glanced at me. He said to Gary, "What is it? I haven't seen it yet."

"It's stupid. Something about feet."

"Feet?" I said.

"Yeah. Thousands of feet or something."

"What's it mean?" Nate said.

Gary shrugged. "Who knows? Maybe it means that the treasure is within walking distance of the *Daily* office. It's stupid."

Nate smiled and threw me a wink. Gary happened to look at him just then. He said, "Who are you winking at?"

"That girl," Nate said innocently. His hair had fallen across his forehead.

"Which one?" Gary was trying to figure out where Nate was looking.

"Over there. In the Mills College shirt. I'm going to go ask her to dance."

He did, too. We watched him walk up to her. She sized him up, gave him a little smile, and said okay. They disappeared into the group of dancers. I couldn't figure out if Nate had really had his eye on her, or if he just wanted to cover up the wink, or both.

We watched the dancers for a while and made a few comments to each other. I began to feel out of it just standing there. There were girls from Ragtown at the dance, and I knew all of them and had even gone out with a couple, but I didn't want to dance with them. I felt like summer was a time for new adventures—a time to ask a stranger from a distant place to dance. But I couldn't bring myself to do it.

I heard some commotion at one end of the dance area and stood up on my tiptoes to see what was going on. I thought it was a fight at first. Then I heard someone yell, "Oh, gross!" I headed that way with Gary and squirmed past some people until we reached the center of the action, the source of the excitement.

I couldn't believe what I saw. It was Rodney, bent over, his hands on his knees, vomiting on the asphalt like he had plans to cover the entire parking lot. He was really blowing it out. People were fleeing and screaming like they do in monster movies. But not Maggie. She was right there by his side, talking him through it, nursing him along.

"That's it," she said. "Let it all out. Let yourself go, Rodney."

Her advice seemed kind of unnecessary to me, since Rodney wasn't exactly holding back. His chest was heaving like bellows. I wondered what had made him so sick. Then I remembered his Miwok dinner menu.

"Wow," said Gary.

After a pause that gave the impression it might be over, Rodney let out a fresh roar and a splash. There was another lull. He didn't move an inch. He seemed afraid to move, as if that might get him going again. He stayed hunched over and stared straight down at all he had accomplished.

Finally, Maggie put an arm around his shoulders and gently led him away, calling out to the crowd, "He'll be fine." He seemed to be in pretty good hands, so I stayed out of it. It was an easy choice to make.

Gary gave a whistle under his breath, almost as if in awe of Rodney, and we started to go back to where we'd been standing. I suddenly realized I was tired. My dad always told me one sign of maturity was knowing for sure what you wanted. Basically, I wanted to go to sleep. I told Gary I was going to pack it in, and he said okay, he'd see me next week. He came up for every Friday dance, just to stand around like me.

It was pretty quiet along the road between the wooded picnic grounds and the campground. People were getting ready for bed at their campsites. I walked by one tent with a lantern in it and heard a man say, "Four letters, Ruth. Starts with a 'g.'" They were having a wild Friday night—crosswords in the old tent. A little farther along I heard some voices from one of the picnic tables—guys laughing and trying not to laugh and telling each other to be quiet. I heard the shatter of glass and some giggles. I figured I'd be picking up beer-bottle fragments on Monday. Then I thought of Nate and the easy way he walked up to that girl. He just walked right up to her.

Someone halfway around the lake suddenly shouted, "Elmer!" The guys at the picnic table picked it up and called it out, and the people back at the dance must have heard them, because they yelled it too. For a moment it was nothing but "Elmer!" all over the place. Then it quieted back down. This was a familiar nighttime sound at Quiver Lake. Someone who happened to feel like doing it would suddenly call out "Elmer!" and people would shout the name back. You'd hear it all over the lake, and then it would suddenly be quiet again. I'd asked around about it, but nobody knew how it started or who Elmer was. It was just a thing people did here.

I got back to the cabin and turned on the TV. The cabin didn't have cable, and at this elevation we got only one channel clearly. It was showing a dumb movie, and I watched it a while. Nate and I often talked about how life in movies was different from real life. We had even started a list, just in our heads, of Fake Stuff in the Movies. But this one didn't have any new fake stuff, so it was a total waste.

I got in bed and read. I was waiting up for Nate. Just when I'd decided he wasn't going to show up, I heard the back door open. He came up the stairs and looked into my room. We talked a little about Rodney's moment in the spotlight, then about our plans for the weekend. There was a pause. He sighed.

"Well?" I said.

He moaned. "It was a bust. We spent the whole time talking about how young I was."

"How old is she?"

"Eighteen. She's going to start college in the fall. She said she never would have agreed to dance with me if she knew I was just sixteen. It didn't matter to her that I'll be seventeen in two months, or that I'll be in college myself in fifteen months. God, I felt like a ten-year-old. The thing is, she *liked* me. She actually *liked* me. And I liked her. But she couldn't handle it. 'Robbing the cradle,' she said." He looked at me. "You ask anybody to dance?"

"Not really."

"You're smart. Less grief that way. Well, I'm gonna go cry myself to sleep."

I said good-night and turned out my light. Just before I dropped off to sleep, I heard an "Elmer!" from somewhere way off. It was late, so there wasn't much of a response.

Four

As I sat down at one of the picnic tables and began to unpack my lunch, I looked around for Nate. Sometimes he and Norman the Foreman joined me for lunch and sometimes they didn't. I munched on my peanut-butter-and-banana sandwich and watched the boats and water-skiers out on the lake. I imagined them trying to do that a hundred and fifty years ago. They wouldn't have gotten very far. You can't water-ski on land.

The lake used to be a huge meadow with a river running along one edge of it—Quiver River. Some of the granite was blasted out of the mountainside above the river to make a dam, which the miners needed for some reason, and the river flooded the meadow. I imagined myself back at that moment. I pictured a meadow in front of me instead of a lake, with a river at the far edge of it. I could see the river rising because of the dam, spilling over its banks and coming my way. I saw it, in speeded-up time, rolling toward me in a wave and coming to a stop at the beach. From meadow to lake in ten seconds.

A group of people were coming through the trees. It was the noon nature walk around the lake, led by Paul Ling, a U.S. Forest Service Ranger. He came by about this time every Monday. I took his nature walk the week before I started work and liked it a lot. Paul, an Asian American of Chinese ancestry, was a nice guy and just a little odd. He took his work very seriously and gave his tour groups lots of tips on how to remember what he told them, as if someone might stop them on the highway and give them a pop quiz or something.

Paul was talking to the group about Jeffrey pine trees, walking backward the whole time. As he passed between my table and the beach, he spotted me and waved. He kept talking and walking backward until he seemed about to crash into a tree, but he sidestepped just in time to dodge it, and he spun around and walked forward normally. He did this every time, exactly the same way, coming so close to the tree that sometimes people in the group would start to warn him. I think he did it to show off, as if to say he knew the woods so well that he could tell where the trees were without looking. He did know his stuff. Plants, animals, geology, history—if you had a question about this part of California, Paul was the guy to ask.

As they moved on, I could just barely hear him. "The bark of the Jeffrey pine smells exactly like a vanilla milk shake. There's one up ahead. Let's stop and smell it, shall we?"

I watched them, in the distance, gather around the tree and smell it. It was pretty funny—all these tourists with their noses stuck in the bark. They looked like a bunch of primitive people whispering secrets to the tree. They backed off from it and nodded. I couldn't hear them, but I knew they were saying, "Yep. Just like a vanilla milk shake."

The group started to move on, but one of them still had his nose in the tree. He was hugging it like he had fallen in love with it. He even had his legs wrapped around it. Paul started to call out to him but then grinned and waved his hand—a get-out-of-here wave. That made me look closer. The guy humping the tree was Nate, fooling around. He hopped off the tree with a laugh and grabbed his shovel from Norman the Foreman, who was standing off to the side looking bored. Then they headed my way.

Norman and Nate were a total mismatch. Nate

liked to laugh, but Norman scowled at everything that came his way. Nate and I figured some tragedy lurked in his past that explained everything, and now and then we pumped him, trying to discover it. He was the principal of Quiver Lake Grammar School nine months out of the year, but that didn't strike me as tragic enough. He lost a favorite horse this winter. It just disappeared from the corral behind his cabin on the lake. But his gloom seemed too deep and permanent for that to be the explanation. He was married, had a couple of kids. I couldn't figure him out.

Nate carried his shovel across his shoulders and behind his neck, with his arms draped over it. He looked like an ox in a yoke. Norman carried his normally—"by the book," as he liked to say. They came up to my table and sat down.

"Ricky," Norman said to me curtly. This meant hi. He never said hi—just your name.

"Norman," I said, trying to match the way he did it.

"Ricky," Nate said, picking it up.

"Nate," I said.

"Norman," Nate said to him, even though they'd been working together all morning.

Norman ignored him and sat down. He unwrapped his sandwich, bit into it, and stared dully at the lake as he chewed.

I turned to Nate and asked him what they had been working on. Before he could answer, Norman grunted.

"Look at that," he said. "Look at those bums with the Frisbee."

We looked.

"Why don't they get a job?" Norman said disgustedly.

"Maybe they have a job, Norman," I said. "Maybe they're just here for a week-long vacation."

"Nah," said Norman. "That blond guy that keeps showin' his pectorals off—I've seen him here since the beginning of summer. He's been hangin' around for three weeks now."

"Maybe he's got the whole summer off," said Nate. "Maybe he's a teacher."

"Or a principal," I said, making Nate laugh.

Norman stared straight ahead dully. Then he moved on to his favorite subject. "They're interested in one thing and one thing only. S-E-X."

Nate and I said nothing.

"S-E-X," said Norman. "It's the national obsession."

Whenever Norman got into this, I grew nervous. I felt like he could read my mind. I expected him to say, "It's *your* obsession too, Ricky."

I wanted to get him off the subject. "Here's a

question for you, Norman. What do you know about 'Elmer'?"

"Bah," he said. I expected more, but he just took a bite of his sandwich and stared at the lake.

"Where's it come from?" I asked.

"It comes from idiots. That's where it comes from."

I looked at Nate. He had stopped paying attention. He probably saw lunch as a break from listening to Norman. I said to Norman, "How long has it been going on? You've lived here awhile, haven't you?"

"Since I was born," Norman said, coming to life a little. He looked through the woods and down the beach toward where his cabin was. I wondered if he had grown up in it. "It's my lake. Not theirs." He scowled at the guys on the beach and sank back into his dull stare.

I gave up on the subject and began to rummage in my lunch bag for some potato chips. But suddenly Norman said, "I was a kid the first time I heard it." He blinked fast, as if a door that had been closed a long time had swung open, catching him off guard. "We used to sneak out and take midnight swims. Some of the guys would yell it. They'd yell, 'Elmer.'" His face had smoothed out and gone sort of blank. "Heck, I used to say it. I used to shout it out just like everyone else." He was staring off, and a smile seemed to be threatening to break out.

"But why?" I said. "What's it mean? Who was Elmer?"

I wished I hadn't spoken. My voice broke the spell and turned Norman back into the dreary baldhead he was. "Damned if I know. We just yelled it." He squinted at the beach. "Look at them. They act like they don't know those girls are watchin'. Buncha phonies."

Two girls were sitting and talking almost directly under the path of the Frisbee. They didn't seem to notice the two guys throwing it, and the guys pretended not to see the girls. I wouldn't have called any of them phonies for that, though.

We ate in silence for a while. Norman fished through his lunch bag and complained because his wife forgot to pack radishes. He was nuts for radishes.

The crack of a starter's pistol made us look to our right. The Sierra Seniors Noon Regatta was under way. It was for folks over fifty-five. They sailed a course that ran all over the lake, all of them in exactly the same kind of boat—a clumsy thing that looked like a rowboat with a sail stuck in it.

"I wonder if *they're* interested in S-E-X," Nate said, looking at the old-timers in the regatta.

"You bet," Norman said. "They're having S-E-X right now."

"They are?" I said.

"Right now. Right at this very moment."

This was an interesting theory. As I understood it, Norman didn't mean there was hanky-panky going on out of sight in those boats, below deck. He meant that sailing was a substitute for S-E-X. But was every physical activity a substitute for S-E-X? Right now, was Norman, chewing on his bologna sandwich with mustard leaking out the edges, having S-E-X?

Norman got off the subject and asked me about the toilets. I gave him a full report. He asked about vandalism, but there hadn't been any since someone plugged up the sink and left the water running last week, which wasn't really a problem, since the floor was concrete with a big drain in the middle. In fact, it made it easier for me to mop. But when I told him about it last week, he got all red and hot and swore he'd put a stop to it.

Norman nodded when I was done and looked out at the lake again. His stare picked up something. "What's that?" he said. "A fire?" He stood up, agitated.

I spotted the plume of smoke rising from the river canyon across the lake. "It's probably just the Stanford camp," I said.

"Oh. Yeah." Norman sat back down. He seemed a little disappointed. "I forgot they were there. Your brother's in that group, isn't he?"

"Yep."

"What's the point of it, anyway?" Norman said.

"I don't know. To live the Miwok Indian life, I guess."

"It's coed, isn't it?" Norman said.

He was back on the subject. "Yep."

"They got boys and girls in tents there?"

"Well, Rodney told me they've built these huts out of bark—"

"College is S-E-X, no matter how you spell it," Norman said. "You can talk about education all you want, but when it comes down to it, it's S-E-X."

Nate stood up and stretched. He'd been silent for a while, and I tried to read him, to see what he was thinking. He threw his empty lunch bag into the garbage can on my cart and began to wander off. I suddenly felt sorry for him for having to work with Norman all day.

Norman gathered up his lunch stuff. He took a deep breath, ran a hand over his bald head, and stared out at the lake. I braced myself for a parting dose of his philosophy. But he just said, "Looks like that fella in the blue cap's gonna take it."

I looked out there. One boat was well ahead of the others.

"He was the first one around the orange buoy," Norman said. "Whoever's first to pass the orange buoy wins the race. I've noticed that."

At this mention of our buoy, I looked at Nate, but he was out of earshot, dragging his shovel through the pine needles on his way back to work.

Five

After lunch I made quick work of Toilet Number Five. Sometimes they went fast, sometimes they went slow. Toilet Number Six was a slow one—it seemed to take the women an hour to clear out so I could get to theirs, and the men's john was a mess. I had just finished it and was taking my afternoon break, relaxing with a soda on one of the log benches at the outdoor theater, when I saw Paul Ling and his group returning from their hike. They came to a stop not far away.

"Well, you've been a good group," Paul said, "and I've enjoyed showing you around the lake. Young lady, here's a Jeffrey pine cone for you—a souvenir of your afternoon in the Sierras. Don't worry. It doesn't have sharp spikes like the ponderosa cone.

Remember my saying: 'Gentle Jeffrey, prickly ponderosa.' Just remember that, okay? Drive safely,
folks."

I watched Paul's tour group thank him and go
their separate ways. Some of the men shook hands
with him before leaving. Everyone seemed happy.
Paul always left them happy.

"Hey, I've got a question, Mr. Ranger," I said.

Paul looked up and walked toward me. "That's
what I'm here for, Ricky. I'm here to serve, basically."
He said this as a joke, but it was pretty accurate. Paul
was always working, always teaching. He sat down
on the bench next to me.

"It's about Elmer," I said.

"Ha!"

"Who is he?" I asked.

"I wish I knew! People always want to know who
this famous Elmer is."

"You don't have any idea?"

"Not really. There's probably a simple explanation
for it, something like a mother calling to her son to
come to dinner, and it just became a tradition to yell
it."

"You think that's it?"

He shook his head. "I was just saying it could be. I
don't really have any evidence." He looked down
and kicked at some pine needles. Then he tried to

pick one up by pressing it between his boots.

"Norman says they shouted 'Elmer' clear back when he was a kid. He's in his forties, right? So that makes it at least thirty years old."

"Oh, it's much older than that," Paul said.

"How do you know?"

Paul smiled mysteriously. He was still looking at his boots, and I couldn't tell if he was smiling at what we were talking about or at his success in picking up the pine needle. He said, "Over in the lodge there are some old photographs. They're in the dining room next to the big stone fireplace. You ever seen them?"

"Sure. Pictures from the time before it was a lake, when it was a meadow."

"Yes, but there are some others, too. Look at the one of the man holding the large trout. There's some handwriting on it. Read it."

"What's it say?"

"Just read it." Paul stood up. "I don't want to take away from the joy of your discovery." He said good-bye and left me with that.

I had one more toilet to clean. I whipped through it in record time. Then I wheeled my cart back to the toolshed, locked it, and walked all the way down to the end of the beach, where the lodge overlooked the lake. It was a big wooden building, with rooms for rent on the second floor, a bar and restaurant on the first floor, and a porch running along the front.

The dining room was being set up for dinner. The lodge wasn't exactly a formal place, so nobody paid much attention to me as I clomped over to the fireplace in my boots. I knew one of the busboys from the school wrestling team, and he was setting out silverware. He looked at me and complained that his workday was just beginning while mine was over. I couldn't think of anything to say to that.

On the wall were some fuzzy old photos of the former meadow, with a big flat rock in the middle of it that I hadn't noticed before. There were pictures of men working on the dam. A couple of them looked like Indians. This reminded me of the story Paul told on his tour about the Quiver River Rebellion. Miwoks who had been working side by side with the whites suddenly revolted against them, and some of the Miwoks were killed in the fight that resulted.

These pictures of the workers were followed by pictures of the new lake. In one of them a big, sloppy-looking guy stood next to the lake holding a fish. He had one hand under the gills and the other pinching the tail. There was writing on the bottom, but the light wasn't good where the picture was hanging, so I took it off the wall and went to a window. The writing was in faded black ink. I could just barely make it out:

Look at this prize catch! It's enough to make you shout "Elmer"!   —July 27, 1883

Paul was right about "the joy of discovery." Reading this gave me a good feeling. I took the picture over to my friend setting a table across the room.

"Look," I said. "This proves they've been shouting 'Elmer' around here for over a hundred years. Isn't that neat?"

He stared at the picture, frowning. "Is *he* Elmer?"

"No, no," I said. "It just shows they yelled it way back then. Isn't that great?"

He gave me a long look. Then he said, "You've cleaned too many toilets, Ricky."

I found someone who shared my excitement over the Elmer picture the next day: Nate's dad, who popped in and took us out to dinner at the lodge. Nate's dad was a good guy, interested in everything. He always asked me to recommend music to him. My tastes were more like his than Nate's were, he said. One thing he hated, though, was heavy metal. When he saw heavy-metal guys on MTV, he said he had this urge to grab them by the back of the neck and throw them down the stairs. I didn't know what stairs, exactly. It was something he always said.

At dinner we talked about all sorts of stuff—the nursery business Nate's dad ran in Granite Springs, Miwoks, Elmer, and old-time photographs. Nate's dad said he'd seen my mom in Ragtown that day, and when she found out he was coming up here, she told him to see that we were eating right. I told him about our fake menus, and he laughed, but he seemed a little restrained. I realized that he was probably as concerned about what we ate as my mom was.

We talked about Norman the Foreman too. I was surprised to learn Nate's dad knew him, from way back in high school. They went to different schools, but the schools were in the same athletic league, and they played baseball against each other. He said Norman was a big pitcher with a fastball that scared everybody. That didn't surprise me, but the next thing he said did: He said Norman was friendly. He'd chatter a lot on the mound, encouraging his teammates and complimenting his opponents. In my experience, Norman never chattered. He moaned, groaned, sighed, swore, and sometimes farted and cleared his throat at the same time, but he never chattered. I asked Nate's dad if he was sure it was the same Norman. He said yeah—Norman Henderson. That was his name, all right. Nate and I just looked at each other. We couldn't figure it out.

After dinner Nate's dad suggested we all take a walk around the lake. I had the feeling that he and Nate needed to be alone for a while. Some stuff had come up at dinner about Nate's mom, who lived in Sacramento, but they had dropped it because I was there. I told them to go ahead without me. I thanked Nate's dad for dinner and said good-bye.

I had something else I wanted to do anyway. When I got back to the cabin, I grabbed a pen and a tablet of yellow legal paper and settled into the rocker on the front porch. It was time to plan the next clue. It wouldn't appear in the *Ragtown Daily* until Friday, three days away, but I was in the mood to do it.

My main goal was to repair some of the damage from our last clue and lead Rodney away from Quiver Lake. I'd been thinking about it for a while, and I decided to focus my energy on the little town of Sticks, about five miles away. I thought of wooden sticks, but that didn't seem interesting enough. I didn't like "sticks" in the sense of "boondocks" either. I just didn't like it. I fooled around with a few ideas and finally came up with something.

Hurray for gooey things, like pitch and tar.
Hurray for paste that comes in a jar.
What happens when you apply the mix?
Stuff holds. It clings. It stays. It _____.

For a while I really liked what I had written. I thought it was the best thing anyone had put to paper in many years. Then I saw some problems. It seemed too obvious. Rodney would fill in the blank so easily that he would suspect it was a trick and look for a deeper meaning. I didn't like "Hurray," either. It sounded childish. Also, I meant "mix" to refer just to paste, but I worried that people might wonder if pitch and tar were part of the mix. It seemed sloppy and confusing.

I went to work on it and came up with a revision:

Think of sticky
~~*Hurray for gooey* things, like pitch and tar.~~
Think of jam and jelly and honey
~~*Hurray for paste that comes* in a jar.~~
Think of tape and paste and mucilage too,
~~*What happens when you apply the mix?*~~
And you'll make sense of this evening's clue.
~~*Stuff holds. It clings. It stays. It _____.*~~

This was more like it. There was still a little confusion in the second line—was the jam, jelly, and honey all in one jar?—but I could live with that. I *really* liked "mucilage," even though I had to hunt up a dictionary in the cabin to make sure of the spelling. I thought the word added real class.

I decided to let the thing sit. Nate came home, but I didn't show it to him. It wasn't ready yet.

One full day and seven toilets later, I pulled the clue out and reread it. It looked good, but I decided "sticky" was too obvious. I changed it to "gooey," like it was in the first version. This way the clue introduced the idea of stickiness without actually saying it. I wrote it out neatly and showed it to Nate. I didn't say a word when I gave it to him. He stared at it and stared at it, and then he smiled.

"Sticks," he said. "Very nice." He said it was especially good because Sticks was at the same elevation as Quiver Lake, so this clue and last week's could be seen as gradually leading people up the highway from Ragtown.

By the time we were done talking about the clue, it was after six o'clock and the *Ragtown Daily* office was closed. So I waited until the next morning to phone the clue in. The secretary who took it down was the only one there, apart from the editor, who knew Nate and I were writing the clues. She was a middle-aged woman who was real giggly, and she always tried to guess what the clue meant. She never came close. As a newspaper employee she couldn't participate in the hunt, so it was okay for us to fool around with her about the clues. I never would have done that with anyone else.

The moment of truth came fourteen toilets later, on Friday night, when Rodney strolled into the house for his shower, said, "Greetings, greetings," and spied the paper in the living room. He hadn't seen the clue and went right to it and began to mumble over it. Nate was fixing dinner, but he was being real quiet about it, in order not to miss anything.

"Man," Rodney finally said as he leaned back in the couch. "I don't know who's writing these clues, but they've produced a beauty this time."

"They have?" I said.

"They've managed to express an idea without actually saying the word for it. The clue dances all around a key word but never uses it. Look at it. What word is missing?" Rodney shoved the paper at me. I pretended to puzzle over it while Nate came into the room from the kitchen, wiping his hands on a towel. "Come on," Rodney said. "What key word is not there?"

I wanted to say, "STICKS!" The word filled my brain. It was all I could think. I was afraid to say anything. I just shrugged. So did Nate.

"Glue!" said Rodney, beaming.

"Hunh?" I said.

"Look at all the stuff that's mentioned," Rodney said, scooting forward and jabbing at the paper. "Pitch, tar, honey, paste. Every sticky thing under the sun, except glue. Isn't that something?"

I stole a look at Nate. He had the same puzzled look on his face that must have been on mine.

"Why isn't glue mentioned?" Rodney said.

"I give up," I said.

"Because it's too obvious!"

"It is?"

"Of course it is. What do you think of when you think of glue?"

At the moment, I couldn't think of anything. I couldn't figure out where Rodney was going with this. It sure wasn't where I had meant for him to go.

"I'll put it this way," Rodney said, trying to be patient. "What's the most famous brand of glue there is?"

"Elmer's," Nate said right away.

"Exactly," said Rodney. "And what does 'Elmer' make you think of?"

"Oh, God," I said.

"Yep," said Rodney. "It's really a clever clue. But I'm amazed at how much it gives away. Last week's clue didn't point right to Quiver Lake. It just pointed to the five-thousand-foot level of elevation, which applies to a whole bunch of places. But now we can say for sure that the treasure is at Quiver Lake." Rodney shook his head in a worried way. "At the rate the clues are spilling the beans, the treasure's going to be found in June, and it's not supposed to happen until August. The whole thing is shaping up to be a disaster." Rodney slapped himself on the knees and stood up. "I'm going to go take a nice hot shower now."

Nate was giving me a helpless, wild-eyed look. I felt sick.

Rodney paused at the foot of the stairs and gazed toward the ceiling. "Mucilage," he said. "An interesting word. I do believe it comes from the same Latin root that gives us 'mucus.' Not surprising, really. They're both sticky. Well, I'll leave you with that thought." He headed up the stairs.

When I heard the sound of water running and Rodney bursting into song, I said to Nate, "I'm an idiot."

"There's no way you could have seen it coming, Ricky. Only Rodney would get 'Elmer' out of that clue."

"I had the word 'sticky' in the clue, but I took it out because I thought it was too obvious. If I'd left it in, he would have thought of Sticks. I'm a fool."

"It's not your fault."

"How can he be so wrong and be so right? He's going to stumble all the way to the treasure."

"Don't worry about it. Quiver Lake is a big place. There's the town, the campground, hundreds of cabins, the woods all around. We'll keep him jumping. I'll write a great clue for next week. He'll study it until his eyes bug out, and he won't get anywhere. I promise."

I felt a little better, but not much. Rodney stayed for dinner—hamburgers. He didn't say anything more about the clue. I tried not to say anything about his Indian meal of last Friday and the way he brought it back up for our inspection at the dance. I tried awfully hard. But I failed.

"I've had an experience," Rodney said coolly in response. "I don't regret it."

"Which experience was that?" I said. "The Miwok meal or barfing in public?"

"You know perfectly well what I meant," Rodney said.

"Speaking of experiences," Nate said, "I'm getting curious about college. Ricky and I'll be headed that way in another year, Rodney. Tell us what it's like."

I looked at Nate. What was he thinking? Inviting Rodney to speak about college was suicidal. It was like saying to the guy in *Star Wars*, "Hey, Obi-Wan

Kenobi, you happen to know anything about The Force?" You were dooming yourself to sure boredom.

Rodney was off and running at the mouth. He talked about registering for classes, dorm life, exams, all-nighters, you name it. Nate asked a lot of questions. I couldn't figure out what he was doing.

I figured it out later, though. And when I did, I didn't like it.

Six

"How about her?" Gary said to me.

"Nah. Too good."

"How about her, then?"

"Nah. Not good enough."

"How about that one?"

"Too medium."

Gary gave me a funny look. I wondered if he thought I was a coward for not dancing. But he wasn't any better. We'd both been standing around for about an hour. I felt like a Secret Service agent or something, as if I'd been hired to stand there and watch everybody closely and not have any fun of my own.

"How do I smell?" Gary said again, leaning into me a little.

"Real good, Gar'. Outstanding."

"The dump smelled like bananas all day. I don't smell like bananas, do I?"

"No, Gar'."

"Good."

A couple of girls from Ragtown passed by and said hi to Gary and me. We said hi.

"Sometimes it smells like plums," Gary said. "Today it was bananas."

"Right," I said. My eyes roamed over the crowd. I was looking for Nate. He had asked a girl to dance—a short, short-haired girl. Everything about her was short. She was cute, though, and I was curious to see what had happened to them. They were off at the far end of the dance area, and I hadn't seen them in a while.

Rodney and Maggie were walking toward us. He, Nate, and I had come to the dance together, and Rodney had immediately gone off in search of Maggie. He'd found her. Her arm was linked with his. The old devil was making progress.

"Ah," said Rodney as they strolled up. "My sibling."

"Hello, Ricky," Maggie said. "Hello, Gary."

We said hi. Gary seemed surprised that Maggie remembered his name. I asked Maggie how things were at the Indian camp.

"I wouldn't call it a 'camp,'" she said.

"Well, whatever you'd call it," I said, "how are things there?"

Maggie said, "'Village' isn't quite right either. What would you call it, Rodney?"

Rodney furrowed his brow and plunged into a deep search of his thoughts. But he didn't find anything there.

Gary piped up, "How about 'reservation'?" Nobody answered him, and he seemed to lose interest then and turned to watch the people dancing.

"We're having a deer running tomorrow," Maggie said to me.

"A deer running?" I said.

"We're going to try to catch a deer."

"How?"

"By chasing it." Maggie grinned. She seemed proud of herself.

"That sounds impossible."

"It is," Maggie said with a laugh. "That's probably the whole point Lola's trying to make." She turned to Rodney. "Don't you think so?"

"Probably," Rodney said. There was another pause. I wondered who Lola was. Rodney and Maggie were so into what they were doing that they seemed to think everyone knew what they were talking about. It also struck me as funny how

Rodney, who was usually bossy, let Maggie run the show. He hadn't said much at all.

"Who's Lola?" I said.

"Our teacher," Maggie said.

"You call her by her first name? Don't you call her 'Professor' or something?"

Maggie and Rodney laughed and laughed at that. It was a big joke, but they were the only ones who got it.

"She's not like that at all," Maggie explained. "She's like Rodney and me. Very earthy."

I looked at them. Earthy? Earthy? "So you're going to chase a deer," I said.

"First we've got to find one," Maggie said. "Then we'll chase him."

"But a deer is so much faster than a person. How can you possibly catch one?"

"We won't. We're just trying to get the feel of the thing. But the Miwoks caught deer by chasing them. They did it by outlasting them. They'd stay after a deer, and they wouldn't let him stop to feed or drink, and he would get so exhausted they could walk right up to him and club him to death."

Behind her glasses, Maggie's eyes glowed wildly. I had a sudden flash of her clubbing a deer on the head. "Sounds pretty tough on the deer," I said. "Didn't you ever see *Bambi*?"

"Starvation's no picnic either," Maggie said. "The Miwoks took what they could—whatever was in season, whatever animal was available, however they could catch them. You'd do the same thing in their position. And Lola wants us to appreciate their position, right, Rodney?"

"Right," he said.

"You see, Ricky, she's ordered us to fast all day today. We'll be chasing the deer on empty stomachs." She looked at Rodney. "How are you holding up?"

"Not bad," he said. "I'll manage."

I figured he would at that, considering the two hamburgers he had wolfed down at dinner. What a hypocrite he was. I tried to catch his eye, but he wouldn't look at me.

"Well," said Maggie, "let's do it to it." She grabbed Rodney and hauled him out to the dance floor. I looked away from them just in time to avoid seeing them dance.

"Hey," Gary said, tuning back in now that they were gone, "you see the clue today?"

I hesitated, then said, "Yeah. I saw it, but I didn't get it." Last week Nate and I had pretended we didn't see it. I figured I should vary my excuse for saying nothing, so Gary wouldn't get suspicious.

"Geez, I thought it was obvious," he said. "It was all about sticky stuff. The treasure's obviously somewhere near Sticks. That's why I was late getting here tonight. I stopped off there and snooped around—me and a bunch of other people. Didn't find diddly, though."

I nodded and said yeah, Sticks, that made sense. All the while I was feeling like a chump. I had fooled Gary, but Rodney was the one I had wanted to fool.

Gary got slapped on the shoulder and turned around. It was one of his cousins, up from Ragtown. Gary had a million relatives in Ragtown. I couldn't keep them all straight. They started talking and wandered off somewhere. I watched the dancers. Nate and his partner swung into view. They were going crazy to the music. Nate was normally like me, a laid-back dancer. I'd never seen him as wild as this.

They disappeared behind another couple, and I lost sight of them. Rodney and Maggie boogied into view, and Maggie yelled something to me.

"What?" I shouted.

"Why don't you join us?"

I hoped I hadn't heard her right. Did she seriously want me to dance with her and Rodney? We didn't do that in this culture. Had she studied so many different cultures that she'd gotten confused about her own?

"What?" I shouted again.

"Join us. For the deer chase. Tomorrow. At dawn.

We need people."

"I'll try," I said, lying.

The song came to an end, and Rodney and Maggie walked off the dance floor and into the darkness, in the direction of their camp. They probably wanted to turn in early, to be fresh for their chase. I found myself wondering about their turning in, and if there was any remote chance, even the slightest little chance, that they ever turned in together. I tried to imagine it, then quickly tried not to.

"I'm worn *out!* I'm *drained! Oh!*"

I looked to see what hysterical female was saying this. It was Nate's partner. She was laughing, and they were walking across the dance floor right toward me.

"You're an *animal!*" she said.

Nate got a funny look on his face, I think because he knew I heard this and would tease him about it later. I smiled and got ready to say hi to them. I wanted to meet this girl and find out who she was. I was also hoping she had a friend who would turn out to be a perfect match for me. I kept trying to catch Nate's eye, but I couldn't. It looked like they were going to pass me by, and I had to speak up to get him to look at me.

I suddenly realized that Nate had been pretending he didn't see me. I felt a huge rush of embarrassment and confusion. I had the feeling that he was ashamed of me or something, and that he didn't want to spoil things with this babe by introducing me. But why would he feel that way? It didn't make sense.

"Ah," he said as he came to a stop. He said, "Ricky, this is Ally. Ally, Ricky."

Ally looked up and gave me a nice smile. She was still panting from the dancing.

"An *animal!*" she said, pointing at Nate.

"We're going to get a Coke," Nate said, pointing to the refreshment stand behind me. Normally he would have said, "Come on, join us," or he would have just grabbed me by the arm to make sure I joined them. But he hesitated and looked puzzled for a moment. Then he said, "Want to join us?" But it was too late.

"No," I said. I was mad, but I did my best to hide it. "Go ahead. I'm waiting for Gary to come back."

"Ah," said Nate. He said it just like Rodney. What was going on? Nate must have seen I was upset, because he got a pained look on his face. He said to Ally, "Ricky's my roommate."

"At school?" she said.

This seemed like a strange question. What did she think—that Nate and I went to a boarding school?

"No no no," Nate said. "Here at the lake. We've got

a cabin on the other side of the campground."

"Ah," she said. Everyone was saying "Ah" tonight. It was like being in a doctor's office.

"Listen," said Nate, "I'm thirsty. Let's—"

"Where do you go to school, Ricky?" Ally said.

Nate spoke for me. "With me," he said. "Ricky goes to school with me. Listen, shall we—"

"And how do you like Stanford?" Ally said to me.

I frowned in about six different ways. Nate was looking a little sick. He said, "Ricky, tell Ally how you like being at Stanford with me."

"Ah," I said. "I like it fine. I like it as much as you do, Nate."

Nate clapped me on the shoulder. His hair fell across his forehead and into his eyes a little. "An honest answer," he said, "from an honest man. Ally's the same age as us, Ricky—she'll be a sophomore at Berkeley. Well, this Stanford man is thirsty, so let's go for some little refreshment, shall we?" He reached for Ally and kind of steered her forward. She said it was nice meeting me, and I said the same to her, and I watched them head off. I knew *exactly* when Nate would turn around and give me a look—I knew him that well. I watched and timed it, and yes, there it came, just when I knew it would.

I decided to call it a night. I didn't even bother to hunt up Gary to say good-bye. I walked along the

campground road and tried to figure out how I felt. I
was relieved to learn that Nate wasn't ashamed of
me or anything. He just wanted to avoid me because
he was afraid I'd blow his story that he was a college
student. Maybe he was a little embarrassed too. Either way, that awful, unfamiliar feeling of shame I'd
had for a moment was gone.

But another feeling took its place. It was kind of a
slower burn at Nate. Basically, I thought it was
wrong of him to lie to Ally about who he was. It was
no better than the kind of thing Rodney always did,
like the way he lied to Maggie about fasting. It suddenly seemed to me that everyone lied, and that if I
was ever going to make it with a girl, I'd have to lie
too.

I wandered down to the beach and listened to the
water lapping in little waves. It was pretty late, and
most of the cabins along the shore were dark. Before
I knew what I was doing, I shouted out an "Elmer!"
at the top of my lungs, just wailing it into the night
sky. A few voices from somewhere sang it back to
me, and then it was quiet again.

Seven

My eyes popped open just before dawn. I lay there in bed and tried to figure out what had woken me up. I remembered a voice calling my name, but it had probably been a dream. The memory of it was so sharp I could almost hear it. It must have been an awfully short dream—just my name being yelled. And it wasn't my name as I knew it. It wasn't "Ricky." It was some strange version of my name, like "Ricky" in a foreign language. But I still knew it was my name.

I'd already woken up once during the night and checked Nate's room like a worried mother. His bed had been empty. I checked it now: still empty. He had obviously done something unusual all night.

I was wide awake, so I got dressed and went into

the kitchen for breakfast. I put on some coffee, which I'd started drinking seriously this summer, and ate a couple of English muffins. Then I loaded my coffee with sugar and took it out to the front porch. It was cool and quiet outside. I set my cup on the porch railing and warmed my hands around it.

I wondered what kind of night Nate had had. Then I wondered the same thing about Rodney, and that made me remember the deer chase. They were probably getting ready for it right about now.

I decided to join them. I thought maybe it was fated or something for me to go on the deer chase. Why else would I wake up so early? One thing I knew for sure: I didn't want to hang around the cabin all day waiting for Nate to come home. I just didn't want to do that.

I went back inside and brushed my teeth to get the coffee smell out of my mouth. You never knew what might happen, or who you might meet, even chasing deer. I jogged down the campground road. I thought I'd be the only one up at this hour, but at a couple of campsites I saw men quietly building fires. I figured them for guys from the city who wanted to impress their families with their woods lore. Don't worry, kids, Dad'll get a fire going to warm you up.

I picked up the lake trail at the beach. It stuck close to the water and was nice and flat for a while. When it reached the end of the picnic area, where the mountain rose sharply from the shoreline, the trail got a little rougher. The steep slope at my side gave me a crowded feeling. I felt like the mountain wanted to push me into the water. There were a few cabins sprinkled above the trail, but no sign of life in them at this hour. The only sound I heard came from the other side of the lake—the clicking of someone's fishing reel in the shadows, where the sun hadn't touched yet.

When I reached the spot where Quiver River flowed into the lake, I left the lake and took the narrower trail following the river. I had once heard Paul call it "an old river," which confused me until I heard the rest of his explanation. The river had worn a deep gorge through the ridge, and what looked like two mountains, one on each side of it, was really one long ridge that had been sliced by the river. Paul's point was it took a long time for that to happen.

Rodney's camp was somewhere along the river. I didn't know where, exactly. As it turned out I didn't have to: I had gone just a short ways when I was nearly run over by a pack of wild college students. They were running like crazy, right at me. I jumped to the side of the trail and let them streak by. There were seven or eight of them, with Rodney and Maggie at the back of the pack. I yelled out Rodney's name, or he probably wouldn't have seen me. He came to a stop.

"Ricky," he said strangely.

Maggie grabbed my arm and steered me in the direction they were all going. "The chase is on," she said. "Lola's team spotted a deer, and she's driving him this way, toward our team. Come on."

We took off after the others. At the lake trail we turned away from the river, retracing the route I had taken. After a short stretch along the shore, Maggie yelled, "Hold it! We're ready to move up. Fan out."

The line of chasers spread out along the trail and faced the mountainside.

"Fan out more!" Maggie yelled. "Spread out as far as you can, but don't lose sight of the people to your left and right. When it's time to rest, I'll give the word, and you pass it down the line. Don't stop until then. Ready? Let's do it! Uwuya!"

"Uwuya!" the others shouted, and we took off up the mountain.

I didn't know quite what to make of all this, but I was certainly part of it, whether I wanted to be or not.

"Spread out more, Ricky!" Maggie yelled at me.

"Come on! Get with the program!"

I obeyed, moving farther away from her. I was the last one in line, nearest the river. Then came Maggie, then Rodney and the others. As we moved up the hill, I worked hard to stay a constant distance away from Maggie, but sometimes a big slab of granite or a clump of bushes made me veer to the right or left. If I got too close to her, she'd yell, "Fan out! Fan out!" If I lost sight of her for a moment, I expected her to yell at me for that. I wanted to do this right—whatever it was we were doing.

Maggie set a tough pace. I kept up with her, but it took some effort. Rodney didn't do so well. He dropped way back, and Maggie, taking her cue from him, gave the order to stop. I sat down in a soft pile of pine needles and caught my breath. I looked through the trees across the lake and guessed we were about halfway up the mountain.

Maggie and I must have been in similar shape, because just when I felt ready to go, she yelled, "Let's do it to it!" and off we went. As we climbed, I became more aware of my importance at the end of the line. Beyond me was the river—or the steep mountainside leading down to it, since the river was a long way down there by now. I began to worry that the deer might do an end run and sneak by on that side, between me and the river, so I began swinging over that way more, to seal it off, and sometimes I'd lose sight of Maggie for a minute or two. After one of these side trips, when I veered back toward her, I couldn't find her. Then I saw her, quite a ways back, resting. She must have called another halt. She was looking for me, but not up high enough, so I began to wave my arms.

Just then someone up the line shouted, and they all took off, angling away from me as they climbed. I followed them, but with every step I took I felt more uneasy about the gap growing between me and the river. So I hung back a bit. I still climbed, but more straight up than the others, and after a few minutes I couldn't hear them anymore. I hoped I was doing the right thing.

The mountain suddenly got steeper, and I had to use my hands. Then the ground leveled off and the light grew brighter, the way it does near the crest of a ridge, and in another few minutes I stepped into a clearing and found myself on top.

Ahead of me was another valley and ridge, and lots more of the same beyond them, all covered with woods. There wasn't a house in sight. The only sign of civilization was the top of a ski lift, way out there, just visible against the sky where it met the top of a distant ridge. I looked all around. I couldn't see the lake because of the trees, but I could see the tops of the ridges surrounding it, which seemed exactly even with where I was.

I sat down on a flat rock and waited for something to happen. I began preparing arguments in case Maggie yelled at me. Then I decided that was stupid. If she yelled at me, I'd just yell back, that was what I'd do. I kept my eyes on the far end of the clearing.

I thought I heard a shout and listened hard. I decided it was just the wind whipping over the ridge. Then I definitely heard a shout. I stood up. Some crashing sounds came from way at the end of the clearing, and a deer suddenly broke through the bushes there—a big buck, with antlers, hoofing it straight at me. I froze, which guaranteed he wouldn't see me. This wasn't my plan, exactly. I just didn't know what to do. Behind the buck, Maggie and the others came running into the clearing. She spotted me right away.

"Head him that way, Ricky," Maggie yelled, pointing away from the lake, into the next valley. "Head him that way."

I was glad to have some instructions. I waved my arms. The buck saw me then. I could tell he was one surprised buck. He was probably thinking, "Who are *you*, and are you with those other maniacs?" He veered sharply away from me, dipping over the crest toward the valley. Maggie and the others broke into a cheer.

Then, almost as if the buck knew what we wanted and was determined to foil us, he zigged back and shot into the woods behind me. It happened so fast that it seemed unreal. Maggie and her crew groaned with disappointment. They were too far away to do anything about it.

But I wasn't. I took off after him. I figured if I did it right, there was a small chance I could head him off and steer him back up. He wasn't heading straight downhill, but at an angle toward the river gorge, and if I shot downhill and then made a right-angle turn, I thought I might cut him off and scare him back up. That was my plan.

I ran—fast. I had run this fast before, but only on a track or football field—never through the woods, not like this. I leaped over rocks and hurdled manzanita bushes. I slid down pine-needle banks. I felt wild, full of the hunt. Maggie and her gang were way behind me, out of the picture completely. It was just me and the deer. Just the two of us.

After a quick downhill sprint, I made a turn and

followed the contour of the hill. I thought I heard a crashing through the woods ahead of me and ran even faster. I came to a log that made me go downhill a bit more, and then I found myself running on a wide path with high bushes on both sides, almost like part of a maze. The path sloped upward to a little hump of dirt. I speeded up and took the hump in a flying leap.

The entire river valley opened before me, yawning like a huge mouth that wanted to swallow me. My leap had propelled me to a flat stretch of granite that hung right over the river gorge. Beyond the edge of the granite there was nothing but air all the way down to the rocks below.

As soon as my feet hit the granite they went out from under me. I fell back on my hands and began to slide. I groped for something, but all that my hands came up with was pebbles. I was sliding on those pebbles as if I had wheels on my hands and feet. I felt like I was being poured into the valley. Soon my feet would be over the edge, and the rest of me would follow. In a panic I flailed, trying to grab *something* to make me stop. This made me slip faster.

Then I rolled. Not down, but to the side. It was the simplest thing. I just threw myself to one side and barrel-rolled until I reached some bushes. I grabbed them and scrambled on my hands and knees up away from the gorge, staying off that slippery granite, staying *off* it. I didn't stop until I was over that hump and down the path, crawling all the way, crawling and clawing the earth.

Eight

In movies, people always react to a moment of terror by going off behind a tree somewhere and throwing up.

I didn't do that. I just paced around talking to myself, yelling at myself, and yelling at God and nature and everything else. I was happy to be alive, sure, but the main thing I felt was outrage. I was furious that a death as horrible as that could *almost* happen, because that meant it could *really* happen. It just showed you how cruel life could be. Here's this guy innocently running through the woods, and all of a sudden he's ice-skating on a granite precipice, inches away from being airborne with about three seconds to review his brief sixteen years.

I was far down the path, and I glared back at the

hump that had tricked me by hiding what was beyond it. I took a few steps toward it, then stopped. I
wanted to see that ledge again. I wanted to see what
crazy freak of geology had nearly done me in. But I
couldn't make myself take another step. I felt un-
stable, as if my center of gravity was way up in my
head and I might tip over. I dropped to my hands
and knees again and crawled up the path to the
hump. I peeked over it.

The ledge was about the size of a diving platform,
and it had a slight slope to it. I could see why it gave
me the sensation that I was being poured into the
valley. It looked like a broad, flat spout. I could also
see why I hadn't been able to stop sliding. Marble-
sized fragments of granite covered the ledge. They
must have eroded from the rocks up the hill and
trickled down, gathering on the ledge so that they
could kill me.

This side of the ledge was separated from the
hump by about ten feet of dirt. It was just space
enough for my mind to register DANGER! when I
cleared the hump, but by the time the thought made
it to my feet it was too late and I was dancing on the
granite. I saw the bush I had grabbed after I barrel-
rolled to the side, and the memory of my scamper to
safety made me back up, away from the hump, until
I felt safe again.

Then I got out of there.

I retraced my steps back to the clearing on top of the ridge. I figured I would run into Maggie's group, but there wasn't any sign of them. I stood there listening but didn't hear a thing. I decided to go back down to the lake trail and see if they were there.

I came upon them about halfway down the mountainside. They were moving slowly. When I got closer I could see Rodney and another guy supporting Maggie between them. She had her arms draped over their shoulders and was standing on one foot. The other one stuck out in front, with the ankle tied up in a makeshift splint.

"What happened?" I called out.

"Ricky!" Maggie said, stopping and turning around to get a look at me. "Where's the buck? Where'd he go?"

I slid down a bank to where they were standing. "He got away. What happened to you?"

"He got away? Shoot. Well, anyway, you were smart to stay back like that. We overcommitted ourselves along one flank and left the other one exposed. You were our last hope. We came after you but didn't get very far." She looked down at the splint.

"Maggie got her foot caught in a snare," Rodney said.

"I sure did," she said with a grin. "A quail snare. Look." She reached into her shirt pocket and pulled out some thin sticks and some black stuff. She held it out for me to see. The black stuff was a wad of hair. "Feast your eyes on that, Ricky. It's Miwok hair. That's how they tied their snares, and this is what's left of the one that tripped me. Just think—all these years that snare's been set, and all these birds have just walked merrily by it, and then I come along and break my ankle in it."

"We don't know if it's broken for sure," Rodney said.

"It's broken," Maggie snapped. "It's *my* ankle, Rodney." She said to me, "Isn't that something? A genuine Miwok quail snare. It makes the whole day worthwhile. It just makes it a great day. Let's go, guys. I want to show this to Lola." She put it back in her pocket and they began to move on.

"I almost got killed," I blurted out. The entire group stopped and stared at me. I hadn't planned to tell them. It just came out. "I almost ran off a cliff. There's this hidden drop-off up there that came out of nowhere, and I almost fell all the way to the river." My voice cracked as I said this, which made me feel dumb, and I cleared my throat.

"You *look* like you had a scare," Maggie said, and several of the others agreed.

"Are you all right?" Rodney asked. He sounded genuinely worried about me—a first.

"Yeah," I said. "Yeah. Let's go." We moved on. I felt a little silly, but I just had to tell somebody what happened. I had to get it out.

It took us a long time to reach the lake because we went at Maggie's pace. I got a little ahead of them and waited at the trail. When they reached me, Maggie and Rodney were arguing about something.

"I don't know, Maggie," Rodney said. "It just seems so unlikely."

"Oh, Rodney," she said impatiently. "You're not even trying to believe. You're not even giving it a chance."

"Sure I am. I just—"

"Oh, drop it," she snapped. They hobbled off together, just the two of them, not exactly the picture of bliss.

The others shrugged and fell into place and moved down the lake trail, headed back to their camp. But one of the students, a guy with a long black beard, said to me, "I would like to hear more about your experience. I'm interested in anything having to do with death." His eyes widened.

"It wasn't that big a deal," I said. I really didn't want to talk with this guy, and I suddenly decided to go back home. Part of the reason was that I felt a little like a nonmember of their group, even though no one had done anything to make me feel that way. They'd all been real nice, in fact. It was just that I wasn't really one of them.

So I yelled to Rodney that I was leaving, and Maggie turned around and called out, "We'll have to do this again sometime, Ricky." I smiled and waved. The guy with the beard looked longingly after me.

It was midmorning, and the lake was swinging into its Saturday routine. The air was still a little chilly for swimming, but quite a few sailboats were on the lake. People in the cabins above the trail were having breakfast on their front porches. It seemed funny that their day was just beginning when so much had happened to me already.

"Hey, Ricky. Whoa. Wait up." Nate's voice came to me like an old favorite song. I turned around and saw him hurrying down the trail.

"What are you doing here?" I asked.

"I was in a cabin just around the bend," he said. "I saw you through the window as I was getting ready to leave. What are *you* doing here?"

"I've been chasing a deer with Rodney and Maggie. And nearly getting killed. We were after this big buck, but he got away from us. You wouldn't believe what happened to me. Are you headed home?" I pointed down the trail.

"Yeah," Nate said, and we resumed walking. "How long ago was this?"

"Oh, an hour. Maybe a little longer."

"A big six-point buck walked right through the backyard of the cabin I was in. Just about an hour ago."

"Really?" I said. "Yeah, that was probably him." I gave Nate a look. "So whose cabin are we talking about here? The college babe's? Allah?"

"Her name's Ally and you know it," he said. "She's staying there with a bunch of friends." He said no more.

"Well?" I said.

"Well what?"

"You know what. Come on."

He grinned and stuck his chin out and puffed his chest as we walked. He looked like a chimpanzee strutting across his cage at the zoo. But then he laughed and said, "Nah."

"Really?" I said. To my surprise, I was relieved. "How close?"

"Close," he said quickly. "Close."

"How close?"

"Close. It'll happen. It's just a matter of time. Last night there were too many people around. We were all sleeping on the porch. It just wasn't right for it."

"So you got closer than you ever got before?"

"Oh!" he said. "Miles closer. There's no comparison." He laughed softly. "Guess what she's majoring in at college."

"I don't know. How would I know?"

"Physical education. And that's exactly what she's giving me."

"Right. And what are you majoring in?"

He threw me a look. "Listen, you do what you have to do."

"Relax," I said. "I'm not judging you. I'm just curious. Didn't she ask you about your classes and everything?"

"Sure she did. I said my major was 'undeclared.' That's the word, isn't it?"

"Yeah. That's the word your inside source uses."

"You *are* judging me," Nate said. "You think I used Rodney unfairly to get information."

"I didn't say that."

Nate looked at me closely, but he said nothing. We didn't speak again until we were almost to the beach. Then he said, "She has a friend."

"Oh?"

"Yep. Nice-looking. Friendly."

"The same age?"

"I'm not sure."

"Yes you are."

Nate laughed. "Okay. She's in college too. A sophomore."

I couldn't think of the right thing to say.

"You can pull it off, Ricky. Ally didn't doubt me for a second, and you're smarter than me."

"No I'm not. Anyway, I look younger than you."

"Not really. Besides, people look all sorts of ways. Last night you fooled Ally. She didn't say anything."

"It was dark at the dance. In the daylight she'd know."

"No she wouldn't. It's all a matter of how you handle yourself. It's a matter of confidence."

We reached the beach. Some of the total-beach-day folks had arrived and were already set up— towels, radios, lotion, food, the works.

"I'm different from you, Nate," I finally said. "I couldn't do it."

"You're judging me."

"No I'm not. I'm just saying we're different."

"You're judging me."

"Damn it, stop saying that. And stop putting pressure on me to do what you're doing. I hate that."

Nate thought about this. "Okay," he said simply.

"Another thing," I said. "You said something almost happened to you last night. Something almost happened to me this morning. I almost died."

I told him the whole story. Telling him felt better than anything I'd done in a long time. I didn't know talking could feel so good. It came out just as it had happened, and I could see him flinch and wince as if *he* was the one on that ledge. He lived every second of the experience with me.

As we were walking through the campground, a pickup truck with a camper on it came roaring down the road faster than it should have been going. We moved over to the shoulder. I was nearer to the truck than Nate, and when it passed, Nate grabbed my arm and pulled me a little closer to him, closer to safety. He must have thought I was having a vulnerable day or something.

Nine

Later, Nate said he had to drive down to Granite Springs to work at his dad's nursery. From there they were going to make a run to Ragtown for supplies. He asked if I wanted to go, but I passed. I was conducting a private contest to see how long I could stay away from Ragtown. It had been four weeks so far—the longest period away from my parents and my hometown in my whole life. I wanted to see how long I could hold out.

I hung around the cabin all day, cleaning up (it needed it in a bad way), reading, and listening for the hundredth time to the one good tape in the place. Nate got back in time for us to make it to the outdoor theater. They showed *The Poseidon Adventure*, where a ship flips over from a tidal wave and a group of passengers try to climb up to escape through the hull. I noticed that every time Gene Hackman made a decent suggestion about what they should do, this other guy disagreed and screamed at him. We added that to our list of Fake Stuff in the Movies: a guy who instantly disagrees with everything, just so there'll be lots of lively arguments.

At the theater Nate kept looking around for Ally, his college babe, but she wasn't there. She'd told him she had plans, but she didn't say where, so he was kind of in the dark. As we walked home he seemed down. I asked him if he was thinking about her. He said no, he was thinking about Norman the Foreman. He said working with him on a daily basis was ruining his summer. He was tempted to tell Norman what he thought of him, but if he did he was afraid he'd lose his job. It was getting to him.

This got me thinking. It occurred to me that I could go to the campground owner and request a switch in job assignments with Nate. I'd met the owner just once, when he hired me, but he seemed like a good guy, and he would probably agree to the switch. Then Nate would be freed from his constant contact with Norman. Nate and I had never talked about this. He complained about his job a lot, but he seemed to accept it, like someone who'd gotten a crummy part in the school play and was hoping for a better role next year. I wanted to do him this favor. I could feel myself moving toward a decision. I hadn't actually made it, but I knew it was coming.

Ally had told Nate she would be at the beach on Sunday. He wanted to go there right after breakfast, but I restrained him because the beach was pretty dead until eleven or so. He paced and jabbered nervously all morning, and finally we put on our swimming suits and went down there.

Nate spotted her as we were walking through the picnic area. "All *right*," he said. A bunch of college-age people were playing volleyball, and Ally was serving. I had never seen the volleyball net there before and wondered if she had put it up. Physical education.

I wasn't real comfortable about my immediate future. I'd figured maybe we'd be lying on the beach, and Nate's babe would walk by alone, and Nate would say hi, and the two of them would talk. Now Nate was leading me into a whole gang of Joe Colleges, and I would have to pretend I was Joe College too. I searched the beach for someone else to talk to as an excuse, and my eyes locked with the eyes of the bearded guy from the deer chase: Mr. Death. He was staring right at me as if he knew I'd be coming.

He was in a small group of guys from the Stanford camp. Rodney was with them.

My feet wanted to take me that way. There were no girls there, but with them I could be who I was: a high school senior. I eased away from Nate and told him I wanted to say something to Rodney. I said maybe I'd join him later. "Right," he said. I wasn't sure if he even heard me.

I took another look at his babe's group. Loud, bronze, athletic, they could have been in a beer commercial. Rodney's group would have starred in a commercial for something else. Encyclopedias, maybe. There were five of them: Mr. Death just sitting there, two guys playing chess, another guy reading, and Rodney, looking fish-belly white on a brown bath towel. As I walked toward them, I had to ask myself, "Is this the group I belong to?"

Mr. Death greeted me, and this made Rodney turn and look at me. I remembered two of the others from yesterday, and they said hi. Rodney introduced me to the remaining one, the guy reading the book. He must have been on Lola's team for the deer chase. He said hi. Then he turned to one of the chess players and said, "Hey, Nigel, what's a loo?"

Nigel said, "What?" I couldn't believe his name was Nigel.

"A loo," the other guy said. His finger was on a word on the page open in front of him. "L-O-O. What is it?"

"Ah. It's what you in this country call a bathroom." Nigel had an English accent, so maybe his name wasn't so awful. The other guy thanked him and went back to his book.

"How are things?" I said as I sat down next to Rodney. "How's Maggie?"

"Not so hot. She had a hairline fracture and went to Ragtown to have it set. I gave her Mom and Dad's number, and she spent the night with them."

"Really? With Mom and Dad?"

"Yeah. I talked with her on the phone. She's really mad about having to wear a cast. She said, 'What kind of Miwok experience is this?' She feels like it's spoiling the whole thing."

"How'd she and Mom get along?"

"I don't know," Rodney said suspiciously. "Why?"

"They're pretty different. Maggie's kind of . . . opinionated."

"You can call her a bitch if you want to," Rodney said. The guys all laughed at that. I hadn't been sure they were listening to us, but now I knew.

"I don't think she's a bitch," I said. "Just opinionated. Did you two have a fight yesterday? You were arguing when we came down from the mountain."

Rodney smiled slightly. "Maggie didn't like something I said. I told her I didn't think it was possible for a quail snare to stay set for a hundred years. Think about it. Rain, snow, wind—how could it possibly stay set that long? I wasn't even convinced it was a snare. I told her maybe she tripped on her own, and some old hair just happened to be there."

"And that made her mad?"

"Yeah. She was really excited about her find, and I kind of rained on her parade."

"A charming expression," Nigel said.

"Hey, Nigel," the guy with the book said. "This character keeps saying he's pissed, but it doesn't make sense to me. What's that word mean to you?"

"Drunk," said Nigel. "To be pissed in my country is to be drunk."

"Oh. To us it means mad. Like pissed off."

"I know," Nigel said, looking up from the chess board. "We know more about you than you know about us."

The guy with the book just said "Mmm" and went back to his reading.

Rodney said to me, "Bill's reading a British novel."

"I figured."

"Good for you."

I let this pass. Rodney had a way of slipping in and out of his role of nasty older brother.

"When we got back to camp," Rodney continued, "Maggie limped over to Lola and showed her the remains of the snare, and Lola said sure, the Miwoks made them with their hair, but there was no way it could have lasted all those years. Maggie blew up and stomped over to her hut. She hopped over to it, actually."

"Hopping mad," Nigel said without looking up.

"We made a stretcher for her," Rodney went on, "and we coaxed her out of the hut and carried her to the lake. Lola took her across in a boat and drove her to Ragtown. I offered to go, but Maggie was pissed—in the American sense—and didn't want me to. Now, let me show you something."

Rodney opened up his knapsack. He was really into the story he was telling. Normally he was never this talkative with me. I knew he was just showing off in front of his friends, but I didn't mind. He pulled a leather pouch out of the knapsack and took some sticks and hair out of it.

"Maggie's snare," I said, reaching for it.

"No it's not." Rodney pulled it back, out of my reach. "Let me explain. When Maggie left, I hit the books back at camp and read everything I could find about Miwok snares. I learned that the Miwoks would set a whole bunch in one area. They'd make a little corral out of sticks stuck in the ground, with openings in it every few feet. They'd set a snare in these openings. If a quail wandered in there he'd naturally head for one of the openings and the snare would get him. My reasoning was that if Maggie truly got caught in a snare, there would be more up there."

"Clever boy, our Rodney," Nigel said, glancing at me. I smiled.

"Check," said his opponent, and Nigel swore with surprise and looked back at the board.

"And that's exactly what I found," Rodney said. "I went back up there where Maggie tripped and found a little stick corral with four openings for snares. Maggie had smashed one of the snares, and in two of the openings the snare was sprung—it had been set, but it had fallen apart, from snow or whatever. But in the fourth opening it was still set. So Maggie was right. They *are* genuine Miwok snares, and she got caught in one that must be at least a hundred years old. They were set up near a rock overhang, and that must have protected them from the elements. Now look at the one I've got. Look at it closely. The Miwok who made it was a resourceful fellow." He handed it to me.

It was a little strange handling the hair of an Indian who'd been dead for a century or more, but I looked it all over. Tied to one end of the string was a thin strip of leather. There were some raised letters on it: "U-T-U."

"Utu?" I said to Rodney.

"I have no idea what it means," he said. "It's not a Miwok word, as far as I can tell. We've got a dictionary at camp, and it's not in it. What impresses me about this is the way the Miwok made use of this rawhide strip. He must have found it lying around after it was left behind by a white man, and he incorporated it into the snare."

"Utu" reminded me of something I'd been meaning to ask Rodney. "That word you all shouted yesterday. What was it?"

"Uwuya," Rodney said. "It's 'deer' in Miwok. It's got nothing to do with the snare." He said this with his standard tone of impatience. "I'm anxious to tell Maggie about this," he said.

"He's anxious to tell *anybody* about it," Nigel said. Evidently I was just one of many Rodney had shared his find with.

"Check," said Nigel's opponent.

Nigel moaned and snapped at him, "How do you expect me to enjoy this game if you keep doing that?" I laughed. Nigel seemed to appreciate my laugh. I became suddenly aware of how comfortable I felt with him and the others. I glanced over at the volleyball net. Nate was playing right next to Ally.

"Hey, Nigel," said Bill—the guy with the book. "This character keeps talking about pulling his wire. What's that mean?"

Nigel smiled. "Take a wild guess."

"I don't know. Does it have to do with electricity?"

Nigel laughed. "Are you at all familiar with masturbation?"

"Hunh?" said Bill. "Not me. Not personally. I've heard of it though."

We laughed at that.

"To pull one's wire is to engage in that activity," Nigel said.

There was a pause as we thought about it. A couple of the guys chuckled a little.

I said, "It's not a very flattering way to put it, is it?"

I suddenly felt self-conscious and thought maybe I shouldn't have spoken, but Nigel's chess opponent said, "Maybe they grow them skinnier over there, Ricky."

"Check!" Nigel shouted as he moved a piece, and his opponent looked back at the board with surprise.

"Anyway," said Rodney, putting the snare back into his leather pouch, "I brought this along because I wanted to show it to Paul. Maybe he'll know what 'utu' means. Or maybe he can tell us something from the way the letters are carved. Is he around on Sundays?"

"Sometimes," I said.

"Hey, Nigel," said Bill. "The guy in my book pulling his wire is named Nigel."

"I don't believe it," Nigel said.

"Here's Maggie," said Mr. Death, speaking for the first time. He had been the one to spot me, too, I remembered. Maybe that was what he was best at. Not too hot socially, but good eyes.

"Ah," said Rodney.

Nigel said, "I think we should stop our game, out of respect to our injured colleague."

"Are you resigning?" his opponent said.

"Let's call it an indefinite postponement."

His opponent smiled and began to clear the board. Nigel didn't protest, so I guessed he was resigning after all. They turned to greet Maggie. She had a cast on her ankle and was walking on crutches, moving slowly through the sand. A tall woman walked with her. Lola, I figured.

"Watch that cast tonight, Rodney," Bill said. "Could be tricky."

The guys laughed. Rodney took this in stride. I wondered how much truth there was in the joke.

Maggie hauled herself up to the group. There were lots of words of welcome and sympathy from the guys. She said, "Yeah, yeah," in a funny, impatient way, but she gave me a nice hello. Then she said, "Ricky, this is Lola. Lola, Ricky. Rodney's brother."

I looked at the woman closely, and I almost sank to my knees. She was a knockout. She had long, soft, red hair and a perfect face. A model's face. I couldn't believe she was a professor.

"Glad to meet you, Ricky," Lola said.

"Hi," my voice said.

"I'm glad you survived your adventure yesterday," she said.

"Ha," I said. I couldn't think of anything more profound.

Rodney said, "I told Lola about the incident at the cliff, Ricky."

"Ah," I said.

Lola gave me a smile and then said she'd walk to camp to get the boat and come back for Maggie. Nigel offered to get it for her, but she said she felt like walking.

Rodney said, "Before you go, Lola, I want to tell you and Maggie about an interesting discovery I made."

The other guys groaned and fled to the lake, the point being that they weren't about to sit through another telling of Rodney's discovery of the snares. I joined them without really thinking about it, and we all ran into the water and swam out to one of the rafts moored at the edge of the swimming area.

The lake water was freezing. It was fed by Quiver River, which was fed by spring snow runoff, and the water hadn't had enough summer time to warm up. So when we got to the raft, we pulled ourselves out as fast as we could and spread out in the sun. From there I watched Rodney talk and produce his snare. I watched Maggie and Lola get excited as they examined it. Maggie seemed especially excited.

Then, as the other guys jumped back in to fool around, I watched Lola get up and walk down the trail. I imagined swimming to shore and joining her. I'd tell her I had some business on the other side of the lake. I'd talk and win her over with my personality. I'd tell her some interesting theory I had about . . . something. But what?

Movies! I'd tell her some choice items from our Fake Stuff in the Movies list. I'd say, "Lola, have you ever noticed that when people in a movie hear about themselves in a radio broadcast—people like bank robbers—they never listen to the whole report? They always turn it off after just a few sentences. A real person would listen to the whole thing." She'd say, "That's a profound observation, Ricky." She'd find me irresistible, despite the difference in our ages. She'd say, "Ricky, there's something about you," and in time . . . .

"I'd like to hear about your experience up there." A male voice was close to my ear. I turned and found myself looking into the face of Mr. Death. He had climbed back onto the raft and was sitting close to me. His black beard was soaking wet. All the hairs stuck together. It looked like a wet rat was clinging to his chin.

Ten

I struggled through my tale to Mr. Death, looking up now and then at Nate smacking the ball around with Ally, and at Rodney getting cozy with Maggie on his towel. I wished that I'd done better when it came to getting paired up.

Our group finally swam back to shore and rejoined Rodney and Maggie. She said, "I've been waiting for all of you so I could tell you *my* story."

"What story?" Rodney said. He seemed a little surprised, maybe even hurt, that she hadn't gone ahead and told him.

"You'll see," she said. "Everyone get settled first."

We obeyed. When Maggie spoke, you obeyed.

"When I was at the hospital in Ragtown," she said, "I could see a lot of dead time ahead of me—waiting for my cast to be put on, all of that nonsense. I'd brought my register of Miwoks with me, and I went to a pay phone in the waiting room and called up all the Miwoks living in Ragtown. I had one question for them, 'What can you tell me about an initiation rite for Miwok boys?' I was hoping they knew about it from their parents or grandparents. I was hoping I'd get further than I got with the Miwoks in Sticks I spoke to last week. I struck out completely with those guys."

Rodney said, "I think it's a drag that Lola can't get any Miwoks to come to Quiver Lake. I can't figure out why they won't come speak to us."

"Me neither," Maggie said. "Anyway, I called all these folks in Ragtown, and I struck out with every one of them, with one exception. His name is Chief O'Hara."

Rodney guffawed.

"Right," Maggie said. "It's a funny name. Actually, 'Chief' is a nickname he grew up with, and it stuck. He wouldn't give me any other first name. And 'O'Hara' is an adopted name. His great-grandparents adopted it from a white family in the area."

"I wasn't laughing at his name," Rodney said. "I was laughing because I know the guy."

"Oh," said Maggie. Rodney seemed about to say more, but she didn't let him. "Chief O'Hara said sure, there was an initiation rite for boys, and he'd be happy to tell me about it. I couldn't believe it. He was the last one on my Ragtown list, and here he was, eager to solve this huge problem for me. He told me about a two-part initiation rite. The first part involved the Miwok boy trying to run down a deer."

"All by himself?" Nigel asked.

"Yes. He didn't have to succeed, but he had to try. Thanks to Lola we know how hard it is for a large group of hunters to run down a deer, so you can appreciate how hard it was for one boy to do it. But the Miwoks had a special way of catching a deer when they were on their own. They would find a high cliff with a straight dropoff. They would cut brush and stack it up into two walls leading to the cliff, making sort of a runway that would guide the deer right off the cliff. If it was made right, the deer would be going full speed when he saw the edge, and he wouldn't be able to stop in time. He'd go flying off and die on the rocks below. This kind of trap is called a 'motu,' and that's also the name for this first stage of the initiation—the 'motu.'"

"Hey," I said, mainly to myself. Everyone looked at me.

"What is it?" Maggie said.

"I think I was in a motu."

Her eyes widened.

"I mean when I almost fell off the cliff. I remember brush on both sides. It formed two walls and kind of a runway, just like what you describe."

"Are you sure?" Rodney asked. He sounded skeptical, almost scornful.

"Yeah," I said. "Pretty sure."

Rodney said, "It could have just grown that way." He didn't want me to get credit for finding something interesting. That was Rodney, through and through.

Maggie said, "That's pretty exciting, Ricky. You'll have to show us where it is." She turned to the others. "Now, the second part of the initiation—"

"I know this guy, Chief O'Hara," Rodney said.

Maggie looked at him. "You already said that, Rodney."

"He's kind of a practical joker."

Maggie stared. "What are you saying?"

"I think maybe he was pulling your leg."

"You're saying I can't tell when someone is lying to me?"

"I just know how committed you are to this stuff."

"So committed I'm blind? Is that what you're saying?"

"Yeah," Rodney said. "Partially blind, anyway."

I thought Maggie was going to scream at him. Instead, she calmly said, "You're wrong." She turned to the rest of us. "The second part of the initiation happens on the seventh night after the motu. It's called the 'aimah.' The name comes from a sacred rock that's part of the ritual. It's a large rock in the shape of a human lying down on his back."

Nigel said, "Was this rock a natural phenomenon, Maggie, or did they carve it?"

"I asked Chief O'Hara that. He said it's natural."

Nigel frowned. "I imagine it would be hard to find such a thing. What did they do if there wasn't one lying about?"

"I didn't ask him that. What is this? Don't you believe it either?"

"Now now," Nigel said calmly. "I wasn't suggesting that. I just asked a question."

"What do they do with this rock?" Bill asked.

Maggie hesitated before answering. "They give it hair."

"What?" said Rodney.

"They give it hair. That's all Chief O'Hara said about it. He wouldn't explain. Actually, I don't think he could. He seemed to be stuck with that phrase. 'They give it hair.'"

"Hmph," Rodney said.

"Look," Maggie said to him. "The fact that he couldn't say anything more about it doesn't mean he was lying. In fact, it's good evidence he was telling the truth. If he'd just been fooling with me, he wouldn't have left it vague. He would have made something up about the hair."

Rodney shrugged. "Maybe he just got bored."

Maggie got to her feet. "You can be a real prick, Rodney."

I'd been telling Rodney this all my life, but coming from her, the words sounded more convincing.

"Oh, don't get all steamed up, Maggie," Rodney said.

"Nigel," she said, "hand me my crutches. I'm walking back."

"No you're not," Nigel said as he stood up. "It's too far. Besides, here comes the boat."

We looked to the lake. Lola was chugging toward us. Her red hair really stood out in the sunlight. Maggie grabbed the crutches herself and said, "I'm going down to the dock to meet her."

"I'm going with you," Rodney said.

Maggie said nothing to this. She just went off in a huff. She moved faster on crutches than anyone I'd ever seen. Rodney got up, grabbed his stuff, and took off. But then he thought of something and came back. He handed me the leather pouch with the snare in it.

"When you see Paul, show this to him and ask him about it."

"Right," I said.

"Pay attention to what he says." Rodney said this as if I was a moron. He took off after Maggie.

Nigel said, "I think I shall be going too. On the one hand, those two lovebirds would like to be alone to sort things out. On the other hand, I don't feel like walking back, and Lola will be with them anyway, so what difference does it make if I'm in the boat?"

The other guys said they admired his thinking and grabbed their things. They said good-bye to me.

Nigel added, "I hope your love life is a little smoother than your brother's," and they all laughed and headed for the dock.

I watched the boat pull up. From this distance, Lola didn't look particularly old. She could pass for a college student. Maybe even a high school senior. Everyone piled into the boat. Rodney tried to help Maggie, but she didn't need it. The boat didn't go anywhere. Then I saw that they were drawing straws. I guessed it was overloaded and one of them would have to get out and walk back to camp. I watched to see which one it would be.

It just wasn't Rodney's day.

"Hey, Ricky," a girl behind me yelled. "Get your buns over here." I turned around. Ally was waving.

"We need another guy on our team. Come on. We're winning."

I obviously didn't have any other commitments, so I grabbed my towel and joined them. Ally made some quick introductions, so quick that I didn't catch any names. There were seven people besides me—Nate and Ally and a skinny guy on this side and two big guys and two girls on the other. During the introductions, I tried to look old. My smile was a knowing smile. My eyes twinkled with wisdom. I probably looked like an idiot.

"You take the right rear corner, Ricky," Ally said.

"Ricky," one of the guys across the net said. "Ricky Ricardo?" His teammates laughed. "How's Lucy? Lucy, I'm ho-ome," he said in a thick Spanish accent. His team really cracked up at that. I managed a grin. I knew they weren't making fun of me or anything. I just thought it was kind of dumb.

"Your serve," Ally said as she rolled the ball to the joker on the other side.

One of the girls on his team said, "Hit it to Fred," and the other one said, "No, Ethel. Hit it to Ethel." They were giving us code names based on the TV show. I was anxious for the game to start, because I was nervous and I thought it would help if I got my hands on the ball. Besides, I hated *I Love Lucy*. Whenever I stumbled upon it on TV, I yelled and hit the channel changer as fast as I could.

When the game finally began, everything was fine. I loved volleyball. I especially liked diving for a ball and saving it, getting it in the air just enough for someone else to get to it. I liked to go all out, and Ally and Nate and the other guy on our team kidded me about it. They said, "Hey, try a little bit, will ya?" and stuff like that.

Then one of the guys on the other team—not the joker but the other one, a real beefy guy with arms that hung out at the sides of his chest like parentheses—started calling me "Little Ricky." I remembered that Ricky and Lucy had a son they called Little Ricky. The guy was probably just picking one more name to try to be funny with, but I couldn't get it out of my head that he was making a wisecrack about my age. I was afraid he suspected I didn't belong with them.

My team won the game. The other team was bigger, but we had the edge on nimbleness. Joker and Mr. Parentheses wanted to play again, but Ally said she'd had enough, and she, Nate, and I found a good place on the beach and spread our towels out.

Ally smacked me on the arm as we sat down. "Hey, you're a good player," she said.

I smacked her in return. "Hey, thanks. So are you."

"Well," she said, "shall we get back to work, Nate?"

I wondered what this might involve and looked at Nate. He seemed to squirm a little. Ally looked at me and explained:

"I've been helping Nate with the next clue. He told me all about the treasure hunt. I think it's terrific. He told me you put it in the lake, but he won't say where, the brute."

I looked at Nate. "Yeah," I said slowly. "Yeah. He's a brute, all right. Um, Nate, could I have a word with you?" I stood up.

Nate was trying to look like he didn't know what I was thinking. But of course he knew, and he knew I knew he knew. There was a lot of knowledge between us. He got to his feet and we stepped aside. Ally watched us a moment, and then she turned and looked at the lake.

When we were out of earshot I said, "I'm so pissed off right now I'm going to have to leave. I don't want to ruin whatever you've got going here."

Nate said, "Listen—"

"I'm going to leave. I'll say good-bye to Ally very nicely, and she won't know that I want to kill you."

"Look—"

"What the hell were you thinking? You barely know her. She could try to find it herself, or blab it to her friends. I know you're hot to impress her, but you went too far. You screwed up."

Nate clenched his jaw and stared out at the lake. I went back to Ally, picked up my towel, and said, "I've got to run. Nice seeing you again."

"Nice seeing you," she said, and she looked for Nate. He was still standing there, staring out at the lake.

Nate got back to the cabin late, but I was still up. He said Ally was going up the highway for a backpacking trip with her friends, so he wouldn't be seeing her for a few days. He had a date with her for the Friday dance, though. He said he talked to her about how important it was to keep the location of the treasure a secret, and she said she understood that. She was honest, Nate said. He trusted her. And after this clue he wouldn't consult with her again. He promised.

I said good, and that settled it.

Eleven

Norman the Foreman said, "Let's talk."

This was always a dangerous proposition, but I said, "Okay."

It was Monday and we were sitting at a picnic table, just finishing lunch. Norman and I were facing the lake. Nate was with us, but he had his eyes on the volleyball game going on down the beach, even though Ally wasn't in the group playing.

"I look at these young people," Norman said, throwing a glance at the beach, "and I wonder."

"Yeah?" I said.

"I see movies. I watch TV. I get impressions."

"Impressions?"

"I don't know if they're true or not. My impressions. I still have this question in my mind."

"Go ahead, Norman. Ask it."

"Okay. Here it is. How many people your age do it?"

Nate and I looked at each other.

Norman said, "Don't look at Nate, Ricky. I've already asked him. He's no help. He just makes wisecracks. He says, 'Ask me next week.' What am I supposed to make of that?" Norman looked at me, waiting for an answer. "I'm not asking about you personally, Ricky. I'm asking about people your age."

"It's hard to say."

"Just a general number."

I thought about it. I honestly didn't know what kind of number to give him.

"Okay, okay," said Norman. "Let's do it this way. How many kids are in your class at school?"

I shrugged. "About two hundred and fifty."

"Okay. That makes about a hundred and twenty-five boys. Now, of those hundred and twenty-five, can you think of one guy for sure who's done it?"

I winced, but I disguised it pretty well by frowning. I couldn't believe this. Norman was a grammar school principal, for crying out loud. "I don't know, Norman. I hear a lot of stories—"

"How many?"

"What?"

"How many stories? How many guys have said they've done it? You can tell me that, can't you?"

"I don't know, Norman."

"Come on. Count 'em up."

I sighed. "Let me think." Stories began occurring to me, slowly at first, then fast, one after another. There were stories I'd heard from guys on the wrestling team, guys in the band, guys on the student council. I felt like I was suddenly surrounded by all of them, jabbering at me there on the picnic bench. I kept track of the guys on my fingers, counting them in the air in front of me while Norman watched and mouthed the numbers with me. He was really into it. When I'd counted twenty-one I dried up. I strained my brain but couldn't think of any more. I wished I had a yearbook with pictures of my classmates to refresh my memory.

"Nate," I said, "name some guys who've said they've done it."

"God, Ricky. Do I have to?"

"Come on. I'll add them to my list if I haven't thought of them."

Nate sighed. Then he rattled off a string of names so fast that I had to tell him to slow down. It showed he'd been thinking about it even though he was pretending to be bored. I'd already thought of most of the guys he named, but he came up with six new ones I hadn't remembered. I'd heard stories from all six of them, though—probably the same stories Nate had heard.

"Looks like twenty-seven, Norman," I said. "Geez, that was exhausting."

"Okay," Norman said. "Now, how many of those twenty-seven guys are lying?"

I laughed. "That's tough to say."

"Are there any that you know for sure are telling the truth?"

I thought about this. "Well, this one guy I know always carries a rubber around in his wallet."

Norman made a face. "Yeah? I can carry a helmet around. What's that mean? It sure doesn't mean I'm an astronaut. Come on. How many can you say for sure have done it?"

"Geez, Norman. I haven't *seen* anyone do it. Unless I've seen them, I can't be sure."

This seemed to throw him and calm him down. He thought for a moment. "Okay. Let's cut the number in half. Let's just say half of them are liars."

I shrugged.

"That makes thirteen and a half guys," said Norman. He looked irritated at the half left over. "Let's just make it thirteen. No, we should round it up. Make it fourteen. Time for my next question." He looked at me closely. "How many guys are there who've done it but are keeping it a secret?"

I looked at Nate, but his face was blank. He wasn't

going to help me. I said, "I doubt if there are any, Norman. Girls, maybe, but not guys."

"How can you be sure?" Norman said. "There could be a guy or two who's keeping it quiet. Maybe his girlfriend doesn't want it spread all over town." He was coming on strong with this point. It seemed to mean something personal to him.

"Maybe," I said.

"Let's add half a dozen," Norman said. "Let's say there are six guys who are quiet fuckers." This word really surprised me. Actually, it seemed to surprise Norman too. He hurried on and said, "Fourteen plus six is twenty. Twenty guys who have definitely done it. We started with a hundred and twenty-five guys in your class. What percentage are we talking about here? Let's see . . ." Norman shut his eyes and did the math in his head. I watched his lips move as he did the calculations. I looked at Nate. He was staring coldly at Norman.

"Sixteen percent," Norman announced, popping his eyes open. "Our conclusion is that exactly sixteen percent of the males in next year's senior class have done it." He grinned. He was just as pleased as he could be. I didn't know with what, though. With his math? With the evenness of the number? With the fact? What fact? It wasn't a fact. It was foolishness.

Nate stood up. "I don't know, Norman. I got lost

when you said thirteen and a half guys had done it. I'm curious about this half guy. Is he a midget? Or did he just half do it? Did he get just halfway in? I don't get it."

Norman gave Nate a nasty look. He turned to me and said, "See, Ricky? It's impossible to talk to this boy. We haven't had a civil conversation for weeks."

"Conversation?" Nate said angrily. "You don't even know what a conversation is."

Norman stiffened. "What?"

"Listen," I said—loudly, and they both looked at me. "I've got a proposal, Norman. We could all use a change. I'm sick of the toilets, and maybe you and Nate have had too much of each other's company. I'm willing to switch jobs with Nate for a while. What do you think?"

Nate almost exploded with happiness. "Geez, that'd be great, Ricky. That's tremendous."

We looked at Norman. Nate had made a tactical error by being so quick to express his joy. I knew that right away. Norman wasn't in a hurry to do something that would make Nate happy, even if it made him happy too. He sat there looking doubtful, but he finally said, "All right. But let me clear it with the big guy first." By this he meant Mr. Lanahan, the man who owned the lodge and campground. "If it's okay with him, we can start tomorrow."

"All *right!*" Nate said. "Thank God! Relief at last! Whoo-wee!"

"Hey, Norman," I said, eager to change the subject, "have you seen Paul Ling around? I've got something I need to show him."

"Nope," Norman said. He gathered his lunch stuff and stood up. "What you got?"

"It's a quail snare. Rodney found it on the mountain across the lake. He thinks it was made by a Miwok."

"Let me see it."

I untied Rodney's leather pouch from my equipment cart and took the snare out of it. "It's made of sticks and hair," I said as I gave it to Norman, "and there's this rawhide strip on it that I want to ask Paul about."

Norman frowned over it. He stared at the rawhide strip for a long time.

"It's got lettering on it," I said. "It spells 'utu.' We don't know what it means."

Norman stared and stared. His mouth suddenly popped open with a sharp intake of air. In a rough whisper he said, "Brutus!"

I looked at Nate. Nate looked at me and back at Norman. "What?" I said.

"Brutus!" Norman wailed. "Oh God!" The snare shook in his hands.

"What are you saying, Norman?" I reached out and took the snare from him. I was afraid he was going to tear it apart.

"That rawhide was on my horse Brutus." Norman clenched his fists. "It was part of a halter he was wearing when he got stolen this winter. No Miwok Indian made that. Some thieving sonofabitch did."

Nate scooted over to look at the snare with me. The letters spelling "utu" were spaced widely apart, and they stretched from one torn end of the rawhide to the other. It was possible that more letters had been on each side of it, spelling "Brutus."

"Where'd he find it?" Norman said. "Tell me where he found it."

"Up there." I pointed to the mountain across the lake. "Somewhere near the top."

"Did he find anything else? Any other sign of Brutus?"

"I don't think so. Just the remains of some other snares. I'll ask him when I see him again."

Norman's rage had passed. Now he just looked sad. "That's the first sign of that horse I've seen. I looked all over for him. He was a damn fine horse." He turned his face to the side so we couldn't see it. Then he got up and walked off a ways.

"Geez, he's really shook," Nate said.

I looked at the snare. All I could think was that if

Norman was right, then the snare had been put together by someone in the past six months, not over a century ago by a Miwok. And the same was probably true of all the other snares up there.

When Maggie got this news, she was going to be pissed—in the American sense—all over again.

Twelve

Norman and Nate went back to work, and so did I, tackling the men's and women's johns in Toilet Number Five. None of them held any surprises. As I headed for Toilet Number Six, I kept an eye out for Paul. He would be back soon from his Monday tour around the lake, and I was anxious to talk to him about the snare.

In the men's john of Toilet Number Six, I made a guy choke up at the urinal. This always made me feel bad. Sometimes my presence in there made it impossible for a guy to empty his bladder. He'd just stand there facing the urinal with nothing happening, like he was practicing or something. Whenever I sensed this was going on, I tried to help out by making extra noise with my cart. The point of this was to make it less obvious that the guy wasn't making any noise himself, and maybe he would relax. I tried that this time, but it didn't help. The guy had to slink off to another john to do the job right.

I sympathized. I knew what it was like. I'd choked up more than once in my life, when the john was crowded and noisy. I knew a guy who got goosed once at a urinal in the school gym, and he was a choker the rest of his life. He *never* could produce at the urinal—only in the stall, with the door closed. Whoever invented the urinal had no idea how complex guys are. Maybe a woman invented it.

As I did the women's side of Toilet Number Six, I reminded myself to tell Nate how to handle chokers. There were other things I could tell him about the job too, if the switch went through okay. I was still surprised at how innocent he had been in showing his eagerness to get away from Norman. If he had had any deceit in him, he would have automatically reined himself in more. As soon as I thought this, it struck me that Nate had recently shown plenty of deceit in the role he was playing with Ally. And yet I'd always thought of him—and *still* thought of him—as honest through and through. It just showed how far sexual desperation could take a guy.

When I came out of the women's side of Number Six, I saw Paul. He was just wrapping up his tour. I wheeled my cart toward him, stopping now and then to pick up pieces of trash. I saw Paul take something out of his shirt pocket and hand it to a little girl.

"Here you are, young lady," he said. "You can keep this pretty piece of lichen that we found as a souvenir of your walk around Quiver Lake. Remember, everyone, a lichen results from the union of an alga and a fungus. Let me give you a little reminder to help you with that: Alice Alga and Freddy Fungus took a *lichen* to each other." There were some chuckles and groans from the group. Paul said, "Drive safely, folks."

The group began to break up. Paul rubbed the blond head of a little boy looking up at him and said something I didn't catch, and the boy's parents smiled and said good-bye. I wheeled my cart up to Paul.

"Hi, Ricky," he said. "Did you see it?"

"See what?"

"The writing on the old photograph in the lodge. Didn't I give you an assignment?"

"Oh, yeah. Yeah." So much had happened since then that it seemed like ancient history. "I saw it, and you're right, they've been shouting 'Elmer' around here for a long time. Listen, I've got another question for you." I took Rodney's discovery out of the leather pouch and gave it to him. "My brother found this snare on top of the ridge across the lake."

Paul studied it for a long time without saying a word. I knew what the first thing would be to come out of his mouth.

"Utu," he said.

"No. Not 'utu.' 'Brutus.' Norman says that's a piece of a halter that used to belong to his horse Brutus."

Paul's eyebrows shot up, and he looked at the rawhide again. "I knew Brutus," he said. That struck me as funny. It was like they'd met at a party or something. "He disappeared in January. I helped Norman look for him. I'll be darned. Tell me everything you can about this. Everything."

That's what I did. Then I listened to Paul think out loud: "So," he said, "if this piece of leather is Brutus's, the snare is of recent origin. It doesn't follow, though, that the horse thief made the snare. Maybe the halter got discarded, or fell off. It doesn't even follow that Brutus was stolen. He might have run off, and he could have caught the halter on something, and then someone came along and . . . made a snare out of it? Why would someone do that? And with hair. Such a primitive thing. Could this be part of your brother's class work, Ricky? Could one of them have made it?"

"No. I'm sure Rodney showed it to all of them. If

one of them had set it, he would have spoken up."

"It couldn't be a joke of some kind?"

That hadn't occurred to me. I immediately thought of Nigel and the others on the beach and the playful way they talked. But this would have been going too far. It would have meant they were tampering with the subject they were all studying so seriously.

"No," I said. "I don't think it's a joke."

He frowned over the snare one more time. "Strange," he said. "I'll talk to Rodney about it the next time I see him. Sometimes I bump into him during a tour. I haven't met his teacher yet, though. What's his name?"

"It's a woman. Lola."

"Oops. Shame on me for thinking it would have to be a man." He looked around guiltily.

"Nobody here but us sexists, Paul."

He laughed and handed me the snare. "I'll tell you something funny, Ricky. You see that family?" He was looking at the little blond boy and his parents. They had sat down on one of the log benches in the outdoor theater and were drinking sodas. "The funniest thing just happened during the tour. See the little one? How old would you say he is? About three? We were on the far side of the lake, up the river trail a ways, and I was telling the group about witches' brooms—you know, those excess growths of foliage that a tree produces to combat mistletoe. There are some nice specimens there. We were in a confined area, boxed in by boulders. The little boy was sitting on his father's shoulders. Now, look at how tall his father is. Even sitting down he looks tall."

I looked. "Yeah. He's tall."

"So you've got a tall man and you've got a boy on the tall man's shoulders. That puts the boy's line of vision well above anybody else's. Correct?"

"Correct."

"So, there I am, lecturing about witches' brooms, when the boy suddenly shouts, 'Rudolph! Rudolph!' His father says 'Shhh. Quiet, son.' But the boy yells, 'Rudolph! Rudolph!'"

Paul stopped speaking and grinned at me. I had no idea what he was talking about.

"The little boy saw a deer, Ricky. He could see over the rocks, and he must have seen a deer running by. We never saw a thing."

"Rudolph. I get it."

"Out of the mouths of babes, eh?"

"I guess."

"That's why things fascinate me, Ricky. There's always something like that. Something crying out for an explanation. I believe there are answers to everything. Absolutely everything. A little boy doesn't just say 'Rudolph' out of the blue. He's got a reason.

There's an explanation for everything in this life."

"Except for Rodney's snare," I said.

"Oh, there's an explanation," Paul said. "We just don't know what it is yet."

That evening, after hot dogs and beans, I asked Nate if he wanted to climb the mountain on the other side of the lake to look at the place that almost killed me. He'd said he wanted to see it earlier, and I wanted to take another look to compare it with Maggie's description of a Miwok motu. But Nate said he had to change the oil in his dad's VW. His dad had let him borrow it for the summer on the condition that Nate take care of it, and it was way overdue for an oil change. I decided to help him. I figured I could learn a thing or two.

As it turned out, we spent most of our time swearing at the oil filter because we couldn't get it off. It took a special tool that Nate didn't have. We'd take turns trying to muscle it off with our hands, our eyeballs popping with the strain. Nate finally laughed and said the hell with it and slammed the hood of the car shut.

After that we hung out around the cabin. Nate had brought some tapes up from his house when he was home helping his dad, and they improved the musical climate considerably. We put on some Huey

Lewis, went out onto the front porch, and relaxed.

In spite of the botched oil change, Nate was in an easy mood. With Ally away on her backpacking trip, his mind was clear. He liked Ally a lot, and if he'd had a choice it would have been to be with her, which was okay with me, because if I'd had an Ally I would have felt the same way. But Ally stirred him up. She filled his brain. Just knowing she was out of the picture for a few days seemed to calm him.

Nate was also happy that Norman was about to exit his life as an eight-to-five companion. He had called Norman at home just before we ate to see if he had talked with Mr. Lanahan. I could tell from hearing Nate's end of the conversation that he'd interrupted Norman's dinner and that Norman was bawling him out about it. But then Norman said yeah, he'd gotten the okay for the switch.

"You know what?" Nate said to me. We were leaning back in our chairs, with our feet on the top railing of the porch. "I bet Norman didn't even have to talk to Mr. Lanahan. I bet he just said that to draw it out, to make me worry."

"You're probably right," I said.

"You're a real human being for doing this, Ricky."

"I know."

"A prince. A brick. A man among men."

"Yeah, yeah. Listen, how's the clue coming?"

"It's done. Ally and I finished it. I'll go get it." He let his chair crash down on its front legs and went into the cabin.

He brought it back and I read it. It didn't take long.

> *I like snow.*
> *Do you?*
> *I like snow.*
> *Do you?*

"What do you think?" Nate said.

"You collaborated with Ally on this? It looks like you collaborated with Grover on *Sesame Street*."

"Don't you like it?"

"It rhymes—I'll give it that. 'Snow' rhymes with 'snow.' 'You' rhymes with 'you.' When you use the same word, you're guaranteed it'll rhyme, every time."

"You don't like it," Nate said.

"And there are plenty of ideas in it," I went on. "There's snow. And there's snow. And—"

"Okay, it's simple. Is that a crime? I think we went overboard with our last clue."

"I wrote that one, so you're saying *I* went overboard."

"Well, yeah, but I approved it, so I'm to blame too. Listen, don't get mad. I don't mean to attack what you did."

I suddenly realized I *was* getting mad. I also realized I was being defensive about last week's clue, even though I hated it myself when it failed to work on Rodney. All that stuff about stickiness—I hated it now. "You're right," I said. "The last clue stunk."

"I'm not saying it stunk."

"I am."

Nate laughed. "All I'm saying is I wanted to try something different. Something simple. Just read it like you were one of the treasure hunters. What would you think?"

I reread it. "I'd think of this part of the county, only in winter, when it's covered with snow. It applies to the whole area, so it's safe that way. I mean, Rodney's not going to paddle out to the orange buoy when he reads it."

"It's supposed to make you think of one area," Nate said.

"It is?" I thought about it. "Snow. Snow. Toboggans? Skiing? Slippery Slope?"

"Bingo."

Slippery Slope was the name of a skiing area about three ridges away. When I'd been on the ridge above Quiver Lake, I'd seen the tower from one of its lifts in the distance.

"You thought of Slippery Slope," Nate said. "Rodney will too."

"What about 'Elmer'?"

"What about him?"

"Rodney found 'Elmer' in last week's clue. That made him think of Quiver Lake. But if he thinks of Slippery Slope, it's too far away from the lake for the 'Elmer' from last week to make sense. How is he going to fit the two clues together?"

"I don't know. Let him worry about it. The main thing is to get him away from the lake."

I thought about it. "Okay. We'll print it. It's different from our other clues, but maybe a change of pace is good. One thing, though. No more collaborating."

"I already told you I wouldn't."

"I mean it."

"I know you do. I'll never do it again, or anything else that would ever displease you."

I looked at him. This was pretty strange talk.

"I owe you," he said. "For taking Norman out of my life."

"Oh. Right."

"I hope you don't regret it."

"Nah," I said. "How bad could it be? I mean, how bad could it be?"

Thirteen

"Ricky, what kind of TV shows turn you on sexually?"

"Gee, Norman, I don't know."

"Come on. You can tell me."

"It's hard to say."

"Well then, I'll tell you about when I was young. Maybe that'll loosen your tongue. When I was your age, there were two turn-ons. There was a real cutie with nice bazookas on the *Mickey Mouse Club*, and there were the Lennon Sisters on the *Lawrence Welk Show*. You know who I'm talking about?"

"No."

"Doesn't matter," he said. "Now, they never did anything sexy. They just stood there. But they were a real turn-on all the same. I'd watch TV and die for them. I'd lie in bed and think about them and just ache. You with me?"

"Yes," I said, though I wished I wasn't. We were on our afternoon break, sitting on a little bench in the campground.

"Now, today," Norman said, "I turn on the TV, and I can't believe what I see. It blows my eyes right out of their sockets. You know what I'm talking about?"

"No."

"Those music things, with the singing and dancing."

"You mean videos?"

"Yeah. Videos. You watch 'em?"

"Sure."

"God, how do you stand it?"

I shrugged. "I guess I'm just tough."

Norman laughed. "Boy oh boy, you must be. I watch those girls dancing and I can't believe it. I don't see how it got by the censors. It's unfair."

This struck me as a funny word to use. "Unfair?"

"Yeah. Because of what it does to guys like you. It's not right to show you that stuff when there's nothing you can do about it. I mean, you're a virgin, right?"

I didn't have to answer this question. I knew I didn't. But I did anyway. "Right."

"And you're not gonna be able to find an outlet for all these feelings you've got for a long time. Right?"

I wasn't in a big hurry to agree to that. "Well..."

"Right?"

"I've got my hopes, Norman."

"Sure you do. Everybody's got hopes. Heck, I talk about hopes every June, in the graduation speech I give to the eighth graders at school. But let's be realistic, Ricky. You don't have plans for this week, do you? Or even this summer, for that matter. Do you? You got something lined up I don't know about? You plan on getting your rocks off in the near future?"

"Not exactly. I just . . . Shouldn't we be getting back to work?"

"What's the matter? You embarrassed?"

"No."

"You shouldn't be. I'm a man. You're a man. You're almost a man, anyway. Can't really call you a man until you get your rocks off, though. Am I right?"

"Well, I don't know about that. I—"

"Anyway, I was making a point. What was it?" He looked at me as if I could help him there. "I got it. Wouldn't life be better if you weren't reminded of sex all the time?"

"Yes," I said. Like right now, I thought.

"But it's always being thrown at you, isn't it? People are always shoving sex right in your face. Am I right?"

"Well . . ."

"Hell yes I'm right. Now wouldn't it be better if there were no turn-ons at all? None of that sexy stuff on TV. No beaver shots of cheerleaders when things are dull during a football game. None of that. My ideal is something like Iran, where the women all wear veils. How can you be turned on when all you can see are eyes?"

"There's still the imagination," I said.

"Yeah, you're right," Norman said bitterly. I was surprised that he agreed with me. "The imagination is a killer. It's working all the time. Even when you're asleep. Ever have a wet dream?"

"Well, yeah, I guess so."

"You guess so? You'd know it if you did. Did you or didn't you?"

"Yeah. I did."

"Aren't they messy? Boy oh boy. I'll pass when it comes to wet dreams. No thank *you*."

I didn't know what to say to this. I wasn't exactly offering him one.

"Yep," Norman said. "The body's a funny thing. It swings into potency when you're around twelve or thirteen. You're ready to roll. You've got the power. But society says, 'Hold on, pal.' Society says, 'It's frustration time, pal.' It's not fair. The whole system's a mess. People shouldn't have any sexual desire at all until they get married, and the moment they say 'I do,' that's when it'd wake up. Then their horniness wouldn't last any longer than it takes to drive to the motel. That'd be a darned sight better than five years, or six years, or whatever the hell it is— ten years for some folks."

This last figure made me wonder about Norman. Was he so bitter because it had been ten years for him?

"The way I see it, the human body is one big practical joke. Nature says to us, 'Here's this desire. I'm going to give it to you nice and early, so you can slobber and twist in pain. Enjoy the next five to ten years, pals.'" Norman laughed cruelly, as if he were a mad scientist, the evil mastermind behind it all.

"Of course there's always masturbation," Norman said. He looked at his watch. "We'll take that subject up another time, Ricky. Back to work now. I've enjoyed talking to you."

At dinner, Nate listened to my summary of Norman's lecture, nodding through the whole thing. He even said some of Norman's words along with me. He knew them that well.

After dinner we finished the oil change. Nate had called his dad, who told him if he didn't have a strap wrench to use his belt to get the filter off. It worked.

When we finished and Nate was drying his hands on a rag, something occurred to him. He looked at me and said, "Hey, has Norman told you about Horace yet?"

This made me nervous. "Horace? Who's Horace?"

Nate just smiled.

"Dancing's a funny thing, isn't it, Ricky? The way I see it, dancing is like having sex with the air. Would you say that?"

"Not really, Norman."

"No? Well think about it. Watch 'em going at it at the dance this Friday night. Did I tell you I'll be there? It's my turn to be dance monitor. Mr. Lanahan makes us." He sighed. "I sure don't like it much."

We were on our afternoon break. I had sat down with my back to a pine tree. I just wanted to shut my eyes and quietly enjoy the breeze off the lake. But Norman had squatted right next to me.

"Yeah," he said, clucking his teeth. "People sure are funny."

This didn't have anything to do with Mr. Lanahan or the dance. He was warming up to the lecture of the day.

"You take the animal kingdom," he said. "Animals are a whole lot luckier than we are. I had a dog named Horace—a damned fine dog, too. I had him from a puppy. Got him sixteen years ago this month. Remarkable dog. When he was fourteen, he knew he was going to die, and he walked right off to do it on his own. It was like he knew I'd be broken up to see him dead, and he went off on his own so I'd be spared the heartache of seeing his body. I never did see it, either. I like to think that dog dug a hole for himself and crawled into it, just to spare my feelings."

Norman became silent. I figured he was meditating on Horace. As for me, I was wondering how Horace managed to cover himself up. Wouldn't he have smothered? And he couldn't have died in the hole and *then* covered himself up. Maybe he dug a hole, crawled in, then pulled dirt on top of all of him except his nose, and he lay there breathing through his little air hole until he passed away. Damned fine dog.

"The reason I bring Horace up," Norman said, "is that he illustrates a point, which is that in the animal kingdom, when an animal is hot to trot, by golly he trots. When Horace reached his manhood, he went on the prowl. There wasn't any waiting period for that fella. There wasn't any social rule saying, 'Hold on, pal. Give it a couple years. Go rub on the lawn or something.' No—he was allowed. He didn't know beans about it, though. The first female dog he tried to hump, he came at her from the side, poking her in the rib cage. He thought that was just fine, though. He grinned like a fool. I can still see him, right now, grinning at me. Eventually he wised up and became a real lover. He'd step out many a night and come home in the morning, his tongue hanging out, and flop down on the porch with a groan and sleep the day away." Norman looked off in the distance, remembering these good times. He sighed and turned to me. "We aren't that lucky, though, are we?"

"I guess not." I began playing with a bunch of pine needles, peeling them apart where they were joined at the bottom.

"We've got rules."

"Yeah."

"Rules that say you're too young to do it."

I kind of nodded. I didn't know if he meant *me* when he said "you" or just anybody. This was a constant problem with Norman. Who was he talking about?

"Now, from the moment it hits you—thirteen, fourteen, whatever—you got two choices. You can do it, or you can ache to do it. You can be a doer or an acher. Right? Are you with me?"

"Yep."

"I can tell 'em from a mile away. At the dance Friday, I'll tell you who's a doer and who's an acher, just from the way they dance."

"Okay," I said. I threw the pine needles away and looked at my watch.

"You and Nate—I got you pegged. You're both achers."

This was the longest break I'd ever been on in my life. I wished I worked somewhere where there weren't any breaks—some penal colony on a desert island. Of course, in such a place Norman would probably be the guard.

"Well?" he said. Apparently he wanted an answer.

"Right. We're a couple of achers."

"So when you gonna become a doer?"

I felt myself tense. "What?"

"You heard me. When are you gonna become a doer?"

"What are you saying?" I said. "Are you saying I *should* do it? Are you advising me to go have sex with somebody?"

Norman backed right off. It was as if I had reminded him of who he was in the public eye: the respectable principal of Quiver Lake Grammar School. "I would never suggest such a thing, Ricky. I'm just trying to help you understand things. I want to help you through this difficult time of life." He was a completely different person. His face and his voice were transformed. From sex fiend to counselor in two seconds. "You need to know it's normal to ache."

"I know that."

"Good," Norman said.

"How could I *not* know it? I'm the one who's aching, for God's sake."

"Good. I mean, it's good that you can admit it."

"What bugs me is you seem to be gloating over it."

"Gloating? Gloating?" His face darkened a little.

"Yeah. You talk like you enjoy seeing Nate and me in pain."

"What's this now? You feeling sorry for yourself, Ricky? That's not very mature." Norman was talking completely like a school principal now. A mean one.

"You're the one who brought it up, Norman. I didn't start all this talk. You did."

Norman took a moment to respond. When he did, he sounded almost sad. "I'm disappointed in you, Ricky. I thought we could discuss these things maturely. I guess we can't." He stood up. "It's too bad. You're more like Nate than I thought."

Deep inside, I had to laugh. This was the first thing he'd said all day that hadn't pissed me off.

Fourteen

"He told you about Horace, right?" Nate said. "You've got that look about you—that worn-out look."

I groaned and sat down to dinner. Nate had everything ready on the front porch: chili dogs with Cheddar cheese. I told him how I'd talked back to Norman, and he immediately got worried I might lose my job. This hadn't occurred to me. I saw Norman as definitely screwed up, but I didn't think he was mean enough to have me fired. I told Nate not to worry about it. I suggested we forget about Norman and go look for the motu on the mountain after dinner. We wolfed down the chili dogs and threw the dishes in the sink.

Before we left, I got Rodney's leather pouch with the snare in it. I figured we might bump into him or

Maggie on the other side of the lake, and I was anxious to tell them that "utu" meant "Brutus." I tied the pouch to my belt and we took off.

Nate was unusually quiet as we walked through the campground and picked up the lake trail at the beach. I asked him about the toilets, but he didn't have much to say. I warned him to be careful not to daydream, or he'd do what I did once. I forgot to yell "All clear?" at the women's john. The lady inside didn't welcome me with open arms.

As we walked along the trail, I watched a guy out in a motorboat who thought he was super-cool, checking out the action as he cruised in wide circles around the lake. He was really on the prowl, looking everywhere but where he was going. This made me think of something new for our Fake Stuff in the Movies list.

"Hey," I said to Nate, "what bugs you about people driving cars in the movies? What do they do that's fake?"

Nate shrugged. "I give up."

"They don't watch the road! They're always eyeballing the person next to them. If they did that in real life they'd run off the road. Right?"

Nate half smiled. "Yeah, I guess so." He seemed distracted. I wondered why, until a little later, when we rounded a bend in the trail. He looked up the hill and stopped in his tracks. He had a big grin on his face.

"She's back," he said. He looked at me. "That's the cabin Ally's staying in."

The cabin was quite a ways up the hill. All I could see was the underside of the porch and the porch railing, with a bunch of sleeping bags draped over it. Another one suddenly got thrown over it, and I caught a glimpse of one of the beefy guys we'd played volleyball with.

"She's back." Nate looked at me as if he was asking for permission.

"Go ahead. Go on up."

"You want to come too?"

"Nah. Go ahead."

"You sure?"

"Yeah. I'll catch you later."

He took off up the hill, making his own path.

I kept walking down the trail and worked hard at not getting mad. What did I expect Nate to do—pass up his big chance? But I was still mad, because I couldn't help thinking that Nate came along with me not to climb the mountain but just to see if Ally was back. If that was the main thing on his mind, it meant I thought we were doing one thing, but we were really doing another.

I soon found myself at the spot in the trail where I

had begun climbing the hill with Maggie's group. But I kept going down the trail. I didn't feel like going up there without Nate. I just didn't feel like it. I passed the fork for the river trail and went out onto the wooden footbridge crossing Quiver River. In the middle of the bridge I stopped and looked out over the lake. I could see the dam, which was hard to see from other places because it was set in a cove at the far end of the lake. The lake trail went right along the top of it, but I'd never taken it that far.

I turned around and looked up the river gorge. I could see a column of smoke rising from a campfire some distance up the river. Rodney's Indian camp. I patted the leather pouch tied to my belt and went back to the river trail that would take me there.

The trail dipped up and down a lot as it skirted boulders in the gorge. At the top of one of these climbs, about a half mile upriver, I found myself looking down on the camp. It was spread out in a long, lush meadow hugging the river. Dotting the meadow were little huts. They were shaped like te-pees but were made out of bark slabs. The huts looked big enough for just one or two people to sleep in. From where I stood, the camp looked like a little toy village.

Lola's red hair stood out from a spot near the river, where a campfire was burning. But most of the people seemed to be on the other side of some trees in the meadow, out of my view. There were lots of shouts coming from there. I wondered if they were chasing something again. I had another flash of Maggie clubbing some creature on the head.

I made my way down to the meadow and over to where the shouts were coming from. As I came around the trees, I heard someone yell, "Ready? Ready?"

What I saw looked like soccer practice at Ragtown High. Two rows of players were stretched out along a grassy field. There were about half a dozen people in each row, and they were spread out an equal distance away from one another. At the head of each row stood a player with a ball, and each of them was getting ready to kick it.

"Ready?" someone yelled. "Play!"

The two kickers sent their balls ten or fifteen yards to the second person in line. This person scrambled to receive it with his feet, and then turned and kicked it on to the next person in line, who did the same thing. Nobody ran with the ball. They just received it and passed it on with their feet. I watched the two balls make their way down each row. It was a race to the end. The lead switched a couple times. Everyone was shouting, and the shouts grew louder as the balls neared the far end of the field. I saw two sticks standing up there that I hadn't seen before—a crude goal. The last person in each row got the ball at the same time, and they whirled around and kicked them at the goal. Both balls made it through, but one sneaked in just ahead of the other, and that row broke into a cheer.

Someone behind me said, "Posko." I turned around. It was Lola, walking up to me with a big smile. I went a little jelly-legged. "Posko," she said again.

"Ricky," I said, meaning to correct her. But then this suddenly seemed very dumb to me.

Lola frowned, then laughed loudly. "I know you're Ricky, for heaven's sake. I wasn't calling you Posko. That's the name of the game they're playing."

"Ah."

"It's an old Miwok game. We're cheating a little bit, though. You had to be a male Miwok to play it, but you can see we've integrated it."

"Times change," I said. This seemed profound when it occurred to me, but dumb when it came out. "It looks like a drill we do in soccer practice," I went on quickly.

"I'll bet you use a different ball though. Here, I'll show you." She clapped her hands and yelled,

"Come on, gang. Time to eat. Harry's special stew is all ready."

This news was greeted with groans and howls of protest from the field. But the two lines broke up and headed toward us. Everyone said hi to me. Lola introduced me to a few people I hadn't met yet. I didn't see Rodney or Maggie and was about to ask Lola about them, but she had gotten the ball from one of the girls and tossed it to me.

It was made out of animal hide, tightly wrapped in a round shape and stitched. I felt like I was holding some sort of alien animal that was perfectly round and very light in weight, without any limbs or mouth or anything.

"It's deerskin," Lola said. "Filled with shredded cedar bark."

I rubbed the deerskin, then shook the ball. The bark must have been compacted tightly. It didn't rattle at all. But when I pressed hard on the deerskin, I could feel it inside. "Did you make it?" I asked.

"Nigel made them. He's a soccer nut. He read about the game and made this his project. He got the deerskin from the manager at the lodge. They had some old ones hanging on a wall they were happy to get rid of." She was looking out at the field, where Nigel and Bill were still playing. Bill was in the goal, and Nigel was taking shots at it.

Lola yelled, "Hey, you two. Come on. Dinner." They stopped and looked at her. "That's not posko," she yelled.

Nigel made a goofy face and smacked himself on the head, as if he'd gotten confused and thought maybe it was.

"Remember the tale of the Eternal Youth," Lola called out to them. "You wouldn't want that to happen to you." She turned to me. "That's an old legend, Ricky. About a Miwok boy who was due for an initiation rite, but he became so involved in a game of posko that he missed it. He missed his own ceremony. It was a costly mistake. He was doomed to play posko for eternity. That was his punishment."

"He must have gotten pretty good at it," I said, and she laughed. It was a deep belly laugh, and I felt insanely proud of myself for producing it.

Bill waved hi to me and went on to dinner. Nigel was bouncing the ball on his knees, and he highstepped with it all the way to where we stood.

Lola said, "Ricky, would you like to stay for dinner? We've got plenty. It's Harry's special stew." I glanced at Nigel. He had his finger in his throat in the vomit gesture. Lola glanced at him, but he yanked it out just in time and looked up into the trees.

"Thanks, but I ate already," I said to her. "Where are Rodney and Maggie?"

Nigel said, "They're on high." He cast his eyes up the river gorge. "They're looking for that rock—the aimah rock. Or rather, Maggie's looking and Rodney's assisting."

Lola laughed softly. I didn't know what kind of joke Nigel had made. Was it about Maggie being bossy or about Rodney going along just so he could spend a romantic night with Maggie?

Lola asked if I wanted to stick around to see the camp after dinner, but I said I should head back before it got dark. I untied Rodney's pouch from my belt and gave it to her, explaining all about "utu." She was fascinated. So was Nigel. She took the snare out and they frowned over it. I could tell they were imagining the name "Brutus" spelled out on the leather strip.

"It's very strange," Lola said. "And very confusing. I'll be sure to tell Rodney and Maggie. I'd better go help with dinner. Come again, Ricky." She went on her way.

"Nice ball," I said to Nigel, looking at his creation in his hands.

"Watch this," he said. "An old Indian trick." He tried spinning the ball on his index finger as if it were a basketball. It spun about twice before plopping off. "Damn," he said. "Too much friction."

A voice behind me said, "Aren't you staying for some of my special stew?" I turned and found myself staring into the ratty black beard of Mr. Death. He was licking a large wooden spoon with stew on it, and some of the stew had found a home in his beard.

Nigel laughed, but he disguised it with a cough. He clapped me on the shoulder and went on to join the others. As I politely made my excuses to Mr. Death, I tried not to look beyond him at Nigel, who doubled over dramatically and pretended to heave, over and over, all the way to dinner. Nigel's show was all for my benefit, all for me, and I really liked that.

Fifteen

The next morning at breakfast, Nate was virginal but cheerful. I'd heard him come in late after I'd gone to bed, so I figured the big event hadn't happened.

"I'm still on track," he said optimistically over his cornflakes. "We had a good time. I'm still on course."

"Right." I wasn't at all mad at him anymore. I got up from the table to go to work. "See you at dinner."

"Good luck with penis-head," he said.

As it turned out, Norman laid off me all day. The only thing we talked about was our work. We spent eight hours doing this really trivial job that Norman dreamed up. At the base of each campground water faucet was a square drainage pit filled with round stones. The stones got crudded up over the years, so our job was to dig them out, scrape them with a hoe over a wire screen to get the crud out, and shovel them back into the pit. It was brainless work. I felt like a peasant from the Middle Ages or something.

Norman drove me hard, probably as punishment for talking back to him. The funny thing was he had to work at the same pace, or it would have been obvious what he was doing. It wore him out. But it all seemed to be worth it to him.

That night Rodney came by to use our shower, even though it was only Thursday. He stuck around for the dinner I'd cooked—hamburgers and home fries. Lola had told him and Maggie the full story about the Brutus snare, and he kept pumping me about it. Was I *sure* I'd gotten it right? Was Norman *sure* the leather strip came from Brutus's halter? Rodney said it was a big issue for him because of Maggie. She was so disappointed to learn that the snare wasn't a relic of Miwok times that she refused to talk about it with him, almost as if it was his fault. She stormed out of the camp and spent the afternoon driving up and down the highway in Lola's car with her Miwok register, tracking down people of Miwok ancestry.

"She's obsessed with this initiation thing," he said as he polished off the last of his hamburger. "She's convinced this aimah rock is up on one of those ridges, and she's hoping she'll find a Miwok informant who can tell her where it is. She's been dragging me all over looking for it. Heck, she doesn't even know what she's looking for."

"I thought she did," I said. "It's a rock that's shaped like a human, isn't it? A human lying down."

"Yeah, but how big?" Rodney said. "The size of a human? Or bigger? Or is it the size of a little doll? Does it have any facial features? There are a lot of questions."

"Is it naked?" said Nate. "That's another question."

"Does it have a hard-on?" I said.

Nate laughed. "Yeah. *Really* hard."

Rodney ignored this and helped himself to the rest of the home fries. I'd spent a lot of time making them, and he hadn't even said they were good.

"What did the Miwoks do with this rock?" Nate asked him.

I said, "Didn't Maggie say something about hair?"

"Nah," Rodney said. "That's what Chief O'Hara said. Forget that. I figure if there ever was such a thing as an aimah rock, it was probably the place where the initiation marking was done."

I took half of the fries from Rodney's plate. "You mean like what Maggie talked about at the dance that night?"

"Yeah."

"The slicing up of the genital area?" I said.

"Ouch," said Nate, wincing.

"Don't be dense," Rodney said to me. "That's not the only place on the body that primitive people decorate."

"But it's a popular place," I said. "Maggie said so. She's the expert on initiations."

"That's right," Nate said. He looked up to the ceiling to recall the sentence. "'All sorts of things happen at the genitalia.'" It was an impressive quote. He did a good imitation of Maggie's serious tone too.

Rodney was half smiling at something. I watched him and wondered what it was. He said, "In one of my courses last semester I read about an initiation rite for boys on this Polynesian island. Mangaia— that's the name of the island. When a Mangaian boy is twelve or thirteen, an adult takes a sharp piece of flint and slices along the top of the boy's penis. This exposes a long raw piece of it. It's horribly painful."

I looked at Nate. He was really cringing and sucking it up. So was I.

"When a scab forms on the penis, the boy is allowed to have his first sexual experience. The scab is supposed to come off then, in the process of sexual intercourse."

"Whoa," said Nate. "A question, please, sir. This kid has sex when he's twelve or thirteen?"

"Oh yes," Rodney said. "The Mangaians are quite active sexually. Every teenage boy tries to have sex every night."

"Don't we all?" said Nate, grinning at me.

Rodney smiled indulgently. "They succeed."

"The bums," Nate said. "Hey, where is this place? Can I go there now and be back in time for work tomorrow?"

"Only if you fly in the Concorde," Rodney said, "and I doubt if it lands there. It's a tiny island in the South Pacific. But I didn't bring this up to talk about their sexual customs. What I find funny is what happens after the boy's penis is sliced. He runs into the ocean for relief, to cool himself off, and he shouts, 'Now I am a man!'" Rodney shook his head. "Isn't that silly?"

"I think they're lucky," I said.

Nate looked at me. "Don't you ever get near me with a piece of flint, buddy."

"I mean they're lucky to have a ceremony. They're lucky to have a clear event that changes them from boys to men. If you live on this island, one morning you wake up as a boy, and that night, after the ceremony, you go to bed as a man."

"What's so great about that?" Nate said.

I struggled to find the right words. "There's no

confusion. Norman got me thinking about this. He defines a man as someone who has had sex. I don't agree with that, but I didn't have a better definition to give him. It made me realize that in this country there's really no agreement on who's a man and who isn't. On this island Rodney's talking about, there *is* agreement. I can't imagine someone who's gone through that lying awake at night, with his cock throbbing and scabbing up, and wondering, 'Gee, am I really a man?'"

"How do you know?" said Nate. "Maybe he does. Maybe he's not only got doubts about his manhood, but he's got a sore whacker too."

"No," Rodney said. "Ricky's got a point." This was a breakthrough. Rodney had never agreed with me in his life. "The culture would dictate to the boy that this is the key ceremony. There would be no room for doubt. He would see himself as a man."

I said, "I wonder if the Miwoks did anything like that—any slicing."

Rodney shrugged. "Who knows? That's what Maggie's trying to find out."

Nate was staring up, thinking. "Actually, I kind of agree with Norman."

"You're kidding," I said.

"No I'm not. Sex is such a big part of everything.

It's part of being a man too."

Rodney said, "What about Catholic priests? Aren't they men?"

"That's different," Nate said.

"How?" said Rodney.

"It just is."

Rodney kinked an eyebrow. "In college you can't get away with that. If you say two things are different, you've got to say *how* they're different."

I looked at Nate. I could tell he was making a note of that for the sake of his role with Ally.

Rodney said, "I think a boy becomes a man when he leaves the parental home—when he moves away permanently to go to work or to college."

I made a face at Rodney, but he didn't see it. It was like him to pick something he'd done that I hadn't.

"There's something else I should say," Rodney added. He took a deep breath and looked out the window. "I don't want you to draw the wrong conclusion from my little story about the Mangaians." He looked at me, then at Nate. "Let me put it this way. There are many layers to sex."

Nate and I glanced at each other, but we didn't say anything. Where was Rodney going with this?

"The first layer is simply doing it. Getting the first

time over with. So many young people view the first time that way—just getting it over with." He stared out the window for a while. I wondered what the next layer was going to be. Syphilis? Insanity? Was Rodney actually trying to lay some sex education on us?

"The next layer," he said, "is doing it well. Mastering the physical aspect of it."

"Right," said Nate. "Let's talk about *that* layer."

Rodney ignored him. "The third layer is the most important one. At that layer there is true feeling. There is trust." He looked at me, then at Nate. "What I'm trying to say is that even though I told you about these Polynesian boys having sex at such a young age, I wouldn't want you to draw the wrong conclusion." He took a deep breath and let it out. He was having a hard time making the big point. But he finally did: "I wouldn't recommend that either of you become sexually active just yet. That third layer requires a lot of maturity, and sex at the first and second layer can backfire."

"Ouch," said Nate. He clutched his groin. "Watch those backfires."

"I'm serious," Rodney said. "I'm not saying you guys are immature. Actually, you're pretty far along, both of you." He kind of threw Nate a glance when he said "both," to let him know for sure he was included. It must have been hard for Rodney to do that. "I'm just saying you're young. If I were you, I'd give it a year or two."

Rodney smiled oddly, as if he was suddenly self-conscious. Then he made his farewells and was out of there, leaving Nate and me to look at each other and say, in unison, "Can you believe that?"

Sixteen

"How do I smell?"

"Real good, Gary," I said. "You're having a good night."

"You sure?"

"I'm sure."

"The dump smelled like cantaloupes today."

"Cantaloupes?"

"Yeah. They're the worst."

"Right."

It was dance time again, with the same old routine. Gary was asking me for sniff inspections. Nate was going wild with Ally at the far end of the dance floor. Rodney and Maggie were dancing too, right in front of me. They were so into it that they hadn't seen me. It would be an understatement to say they stood out. Maggie was in her ankle cast. She'd keep her good foot rooted to one spot and sort of dance all around it, like it was a Maypole or something. Meanwhile, Rodney wore a backpack, which jerked from side to side with every lunge he made. I'd never seen two people so oblivious to how they looked.

There was one new feature to tonight's dance: Norman the Foreman. He'd been here when Nate and I arrived, leaning against a tree at the edge of the dance floor. His bald head stood out and caught my eye right away. He gave me a nod, but it was brisk, as if he was a plainclothes cop and didn't want me to blow his cover.

"Ricky!" Maggie yelled to me. She was still dancing. "Don't go away. I need to talk to you."

I gave her an "okay" sign.

"Hey," Rodney yelled to me. "You seen Paul?"

"No," I called out.

"He's got something of mine. If you see him let me know."

I didn't say anything. I didn't particularly feel like being Rodney's scout.

"If you're nice to me, I'll tell you what he's got," Rodney yelled.

I didn't say anything to this either. He seemed unusually cocky tonight. I turned away to watch other people dance. One of them, a tall blonde in a halter top, invited watching. She liked to shimmy. Her breasts did remarkable things every time she did. I looked at Norman. He was watching her too.

Rodney swung around in a complicated move that was ugly, judged as a dance step, but it did succeed in bringing him closer to me. "You seen the clue yet?" he said.

"No, I haven't," I said.

"I solved it." He grinned proudly. "I solved the whole thing. I know where the treasure is. If I tell you and you find it, you've got to give it all to me. Agreed?"

"Sure," I managed to say. I was a little nervous. Could he have *really* solved it?

"Wanna hear it?"

"Yeah."

He blared out the clue from the dance floor, wiggling his body the whole time: "I like snow. Do you? I like snow. Do you?" Not only was the suspense killing me, but *he* was killing me. I hoped anybody who was watching wouldn't be able to see the family resemblance between us.

Maggie had settled down to a slow groove, with no movement of the feet. Rodney slowed down to match her. He signaled to me to come closer, away from Gary. "Snow," he said.

"What about it?"

"The key word is 'snow.'"

"Okay. I'll buy that." This was hardly a break-through.

"What do you do with snow?"

I shrugged. "Make snowballs."

Rodney screwed up his face impatiently. "What do you do *on* it?"

"Piss?" I said. He didn't like that, so I said, "Ski?"

"Good. And where do you ski around here?"

I couldn't fake a wrong guess. There was only one answer. "Slippery Slope."

"Good again." He looked at Maggie and shouted, "The boy's got some of his brother's brains." He looked back at me. "Now, what part of Slippery Slope does the clue refer to?"

"I don't know."

"Come on. It's got to refer to some specific part. Slippery Slope is a huge ridge. Answer me this. In one word, how would you describe the poetic style of the clue?"

"Dumb."

Rodney frowned. "I wouldn't put it that way. You're too negative. I would say 'childlike.' It's written in the style of a poem for children."

"Okay. So what?"

Rodney gave me a little smirk to let me know that

the next stage of his reasoning was especially brilliant. "What animal do you think of when you think of stories and poems for little children?"

"I never think about them."

"Sure you do."

"I'm telling you I don't."

"Well think about them now," he snapped.

"Okay. Dinosaurs."

Rodney threw his hands out in disgust. "Cheez, you don't know anything, do you? Bunnies, man! Children's books are crawling with bunnies."

"So what?"

"What do you call the beginner's slope for skiers?"

"The 'bunny slope.'"

Rodney grinned like the fool that he was.

"You mean," I said, trying to put the preposterous pieces together, "you're saying the clue is written in a simple style to make you think of kids' books, and since kids' books have bunnies in them, the treasure's on the bunny slope?"

"Precisely," Rodney said. "I'm going over there tomorrow to check it out."

"Good luck," I said. Rodney needed a sign hung around his neck reading "Danger: Mind at Work."

"The earlier clues support my interpretation," he went on. There was no stopping him. "Remember how I found 'Elmer' in last week's clue?"

"I'll never forget that."

"Well, think of Elmer Fudd. Who's his main enemy?"

"No, Rodney," I said. "Don't do this. Don't do this to yourself."

"Bugs Bunny!" he said triumphantly. "There are bunnies all over the clues, so I'm off to the bunny slope tomorrow." He spun away from me and moved in closer to Maggie.

I could see Nate at the other end of the floor. I hurried over to him and dragged him off, with Ally following. I had to tell them the whole thing and get it out of my brain before it destroyed the wiring up there. Nate's mouth opened wider and wider with every word I said. Ally giggled and grabbed his arm while I talked. When I finished, Nate shook his head in disbelief.

"Beyond my wildest dreams," he said. "Rodney fell for it like a maniac. He took it places I never dreamed of. Geez, Ricky. If we keep this up, next week he'll be looking for it on the moon."

I left them there laughing and went back to where Gary was still standing—my faithful companion. We watched the dancers. The blonde in the halter top was still going at it. She had moved in on her partner and was doing some moves that looked like simulated sex. It reminded me of Norman's definition of dancing: "having sex with the air." I looked at him. His eyes were riveted on her.

Rodney and Maggie were taking a break. Maggie pulled Rodney over to me. She said, "Ricky, you know that dropoff on top of the mountain you told us about?"

"Yeah?"

"We can't find it. We've been looking for it, to see if it's a motu. Where is it?"

Rodney said, "It's probably not a motu anyway."

I ignored this and said to Maggie, "It's hard to describe where it is. I've been meaning to go back there. I'll take you with me and show you."

"Great," Maggie said. She turned to Rodney, "Tell Ricky what we found on the mountain this morning."

"Maybe I will," Rodney said, "and maybe I won't."

"Why don't you take that backpack off?" I said. His attitude was getting to me.

"Good idea," Rodney said, slipping out of it. "Would you hold it for me?"

"No."

"Come on." He held it out for me. "You're not dancing."

This made me mad. "Look, what possessed you to bring a backpack to a dance? You brought it, so you hold it."

"Ah. There's Paul," Rodney said, looking past me. I turned around and saw him coming our way with a brown grocery bag in his arms. Someone he knew stopped him, and they started talking. He waved to Rodney to let him know he'd seen him and would join him soon.

"We found something up there," Maggie said, pointing across the lake. She had given up on Rodney telling me. "Two ridges over. We've been looking for the aimah. Remember what the aimah is?"

"Sure," I said. "Did you find it?"

"No, no. We've just been looking. We figure it must be high on a ridge, because that's where the most interesting rock formations are. Besides, the motu is always up high, so the aimah probably is too."

"How can you do all this exploring with that cast?"

"She's amazing," Rodney said.

Maggie smiled. "Anyway, this morning we were two ridges over, just Rodney and me, prowling around these rocks, and all of a sudden we stumbled on a hut. It's made out of bark slabs, like the ones we've built. When I saw it I stopped in my tracks and just stared at it. I couldn't believe it." She looked at Rodney. "*We* couldn't believe it."

"It was something," Rodney said. He kept looking

toward Paul impatiently.

"It was like coming upon a ghost town," Maggie said. "Or a Roman ruin. You could just feel the presence of spirits or something. It was thrilling."

"Is it the real thing?" I said. "A real Miwok hut?"

"No doubt about it," Rodney said.

"How big is it?"

Maggie said, "About six feet tall and six feet across."

"Anything in it?"

Maggie and Rodney smiled at each other. Maggie said, "No, not *in* it. But we found something *on* it—something stuck in the roof. Lola wasn't around when we got back, so when we came in tonight, we took it to Paul's office at the ranger station. He took it to do some investigating. We're anxious to see what he has to say."

Paul finally got to us. He seemed excited. "It's a Miwok quiver all right," he said as he carefully took it out of the bag. "No doubt about it." He held it up and admired it. "This hide is the darnedest thing. It's so well preserved. You said you found this in the roof of the hut?"

"Right," said Rodney. "It was wedged between two slabs, as if it was put there to stop a leak."

"Can I see it?" I said.

Paul gently handed it to me and said, "Maybe it's

been treated in some way. It's puzzling. And if this is deerskin, the color means it's a rare case of albinism. At any rate, the stitching is Miwok in style. A friend of mine up the highway has a Miwok quiver. This one is very similar to his. It's cruder than his, but it's better preserved. It's quite a find."

My idea of what a quiver looked like came from when Rodney and I were little kids and we each had a bow-and-arrow set. We'd take them up the hill from our house and shoot at an old shed up there, sometimes even hitting it. Rodney carried his arrows in a clip-on thing attached to his bow, while I had a quiver—a brown vinyl cylinder painted with yellow jagged stripes. I thought it was the most special thing in the world, even though some factory probably cranked them out at about ten thousand per hour. The quiver in my hands now was crude by comparison. It was made out of a dirty white hide with brown splotches on it, and the stitching was riddled with gaps. Any Indian who used it would have lost all his arrows before he had a chance to shoot them.

"What are you turning your nose up for?" Rodney said.

"It's kind of funky," I said.

Rodney looked hugely irritated. He took the quiver from me. Just then I noticed something big moving slowly across the dance floor. It was Norman the Foreman. He was walking right through the dancers, in the direction of the blonde in the halter top, who was shimmying away. I couldn't imagine what he had in mind. He brushed by her. He was coming toward us. He looked possessed. He kept coming and bumped into Rodney from behind, almost as if he didn't see him. Rodney said, "Hey," in a peeved, high-voiced way and whirled around. Norman reached out with both hands and grabbed the quiver right out of his hands. Rodney said, "Hey," in an even higher voice, and he reached to take it back. But something in Norman's face made him stop.

Norman looked anguished, overwhelmed by grief. He stared at the quiver with aching eyes and let out a loud, pitiful lament:

"Horace!" he cried. "Horace!"

Seventeen

"The thing is," said Paul, "the Miwoks actually used dog skin for quivers. It's just the kind of thing they would do."

"What do you mean '*would* do'?" Maggie said suspiciously. "Why not *did* do? Why couldn't a Miwok have made this?"

Paul said, "What Miwok then? What Miwok? Introduce me."

This was about the third time we had come around to this point. We were all at the cabin—Paul, Maggie, Rodney, and me—and it was after midnight. At the dance, when Norman identified the quiver hide as that of his long-lost dog Horace, things fell apart fast. He got into a grabbing match with Rodney over the quiver, which he finally won.

He stormed off through the crowd, hugging the quiver to his chest—hugging his dog, too, I guess you could say. Rodney screamed at him, "You're tampering with a precious artifact!", but somehow this failed to stop him dead in his tracks. Rodney said, "Who in the hell is Horace?" I explained and we started discussing it. But the noise of the dance made it hard to talk, so I suggested we come to the cabin.

I poured more coffee. We were on our second pot. Maggie declined with a brusque wave of her hand. She was mad. She was convinced she had found the real thing up on that ridge, and Paul kept shooting her down. Right now she was glaring at him.

"Perhaps it would be helpful," Paul said, "if we went over the possibilities." He was trying hard to be open, to be fair. But in his own quiet way he was as opinionated as Maggie. "First, let's look at the facts. We have two objects, a snare and a quiver, that appear to be of Miwok origin, but they are made of recent materials."

"Let's not be so quick to call those facts," Maggie said. "We don't know for sure that that rawhide strip spelled 'Brutus.' We don't know for sure that the quiver was made out of Horace."

Paul nodded calmly, trying to see her point. "No, we don't know for sure. But it's almost certain.

Norman would know his own halter. He would know his own dog. And I knew Horace too. The markings are the same."

"If you knew him, how come you didn't recognize him?" Maggie said. "You didn't say it was Horace until Norman did."

Paul wasn't disturbed by this. "A dog's skin was the last thing I had in mind. If I were the animal's owner, it would be different. The recognition would be instant."

Maggie made an unhappy face, but she didn't say anything.

"Now," said Paul, scooting forward onto the edge of his chair. "Who could have made these? It's just the kind of thing your class is doing, isn't it, Maggie? Rodney?"

"Yes, it is," said Rodney.

"But you say it's impossible that one of them did it," Paul said.

"Impossible," Rodney said. "Why would they do it and keep it a secret? Besides, Horace disappeared two years ago. Right?"

I said, "Could there have been another class like yours, two years ago, or last year, from some other college?"

Rodney shrugged. Paul said, "I doubt it, Ricky. I've been working here every summer for the past six years. I would have heard of it." He looked at Rodney again, then at Maggie. "The only explanation I see," he said, "is that there's someone up there who's keeping the Miwok traditions alive. It could be some Indian buff doing it for the fun of it, or . . . ." His voice trailed off.

"Or what?" I said.

Paul made a funny face. "Or it's a lunatic who thinks he's an Indian."

"*Or,*" Maggie said. Just like that—nothing but "Or." We all looked at her. "Or it's a real Miwok," she said.

Paul frowned. "You mean someone with Miwok blood. Someone who lives in Sticks or Ragtown or somewhere and comes up here periodically to practice the old customs."

"No."

"No?" said Paul.

"I mean a *real* Miwok. One who's living in the wild. One who's lived in the wild all his life."

"I see," said Paul. "And how old is this Miwok? A hundred and twenty?"

Maggie wasn't flustered by this. "He wouldn't have to be that old. He—or she—could be fifty or sixty."

"Fifty or sixty," Paul said, not really mocking her but not agreeing with her either. "He didn't raise himself, I assume. He didn't give birth to himself. He would have to come from a whole group that stayed in the wild long after the area was settled by whites. How do you explain that no one ever saw them?"

"There's a lot of land up there," Maggie said. "A lot of places where nobody ever goes."

"And how do you explain that they chose to stay away from civilization? Every Miwok living in this century has been absorbed into modern society. What made this group hold out?"

"I don't know," Maggie said. "But haven't you heard of Ishi?"

"Of course I've heard of Ishi," Paul said. There was a little fire in his voice that I'd never heard before. "Ishi's got nothing to do with this."

"Yes he does," Maggie said.

"Do you know when he was discovered?" Paul said. "Do you?"

"Excuse me," I said. "Who's Ishi?"

All three of them spoke at once. Rodney won. "Ishi was the last California Indian to live in the wild," he said.

"Actually," said Paul, "he was the last Indian in the whole country to live in the wild."

"Excluding Alaska," Maggie snapped. She got him there.

"Right," said Paul.

Rodney said, "They found him in northern California."

"In Oroville, to be exact," said Maggie.

"Right," said Rodney."And the year was, um..."

"It was 1911," said Paul. He looked at Maggie. "That's a long time ago."

"I know," she said calmly.

"Was he a Miwok?" I asked.

"No," Rodney said. "He was . . . um . . ."

Maggie bailed him out. "He was a Yana Indian from the Yahi territory."

"Right," said Rodney. I thought it was kind of funny that he had won the little contest to tell me about Ishi, but he knew the least about him.

"And how old was Ishi?" Paul said. I could tell from the way he asked it that he knew.

Rodney paused to give this some serious thought.

Maggie said, "Nobody knew for sure, but he appeared to be in his fifties."

"Exactly," said Paul. "He was in his fifties and he was found in 1911. The last Indian in the lower forty-eight states to be found living in the wild. And here we are in the 1990's, and you're suggesting that there's been another gang out there all this time, keeping to themselves and surviving God-knows-how."

"There are ways to survive," Maggie said. "There are plants and animals in the wild. The Miwoks managed to do it for thousands of years before the whites came. And when their land was taken away, they resorted to theft. A starving Miwok would steal a domestic animal from a white household, and a gang of vigilantes would wipe out a Miwok village in retaliation. But it was those same whites who had caused the Miwoks to starve in the first place, by taking away the land where they got their food."

"You're preaching, Maggie," Rodney said.

"What's that supposed to mean?" she snapped.

"Nothing," he said, backing right off.

"I'm making an important point," she said. "Brutus and Horace were stolen as food, just like in the old days." She looked at Paul. "The last two winters here have been hard. They came early, which cuts down on the food going into winter storage. What time of year did Brutus disappear?"

Paul said, "January."

"How about Horace?"

Paul had to think about it a moment. "I believe that was in January too. The previous year."

"There you are," Maggie said. "Right when food is scarcest. Right when they're the hungriest."

Paul was silent for a while. "I grant you I can't explain the disappearance of those animals. That's what worries me."

"Worries you?" I said.

"Yes. To my mind it increases the possibility that whoever is up there is a madman. What sane person would deliberately choose a primitive lifestyle that requires him to steal and kill other people's animals?"

"So what do you suggest?" Maggie asked sarcastically. "You want to put together a band of vigilantes and go hunt him up, just to be on the safe side?"

"That's not fair," Paul said loudly. He was pointing a finger at Maggie. "I'm simply trying to be reasonable about this, and you're implying I'm a racist or something."

Maggie looked a little sheepish. This was a first, in my experience of her. "I'm sorry," she said.

Paul forged ahead almost as if nothing had happened. "How do you judge if a theory is good or bad? You look at the nagging questions it fails to answer. To my mind, Maggie, the nagging question in your theory is how a whole group of Indians in the wild could go undetected all that time. I'll grant you the slim possibility that a solitary Indian could escape notice, but then you've got the even worse nagging question of how old he would have to be. A lone Indian is clearly impossible."

Maggie didn't say anything. I said, "Are there nagging questions in your theory, Paul?"

He gave me a funny smile, kind of a sick one. "My explanation is that there's a madman up there in the hills. The only nagging question I have is this: How dangerous is he?"

I thought Maggie was going to get mad again, but she didn't. She just looked at the floor.

Paul stood up. "I've got to get home. I'm giving a tour at Douglas Flat early in the morning." He looked at Maggie's cast. "How are you getting back to camp?"

"I'll walk," she said.

"You can't do that," Rodney said. "You're really overdoing it on that thing. You're going to wear that cast right out."

"Don't be such a mother hen," Maggie snapped at him. "The boat's gone back. We'll walk."

I wondered if I should offer Maggie the couch for the night. Or Nate's bed. He still wasn't home, and if his dreams came true tonight, he wouldn't be for some time. But I felt awkward about suggesting this. What about Rodney? Would he stay here too? With Maggie? In her arms? I didn't want to get into that.

"Tell you what," said Paul. "You can use my rowboat. No one's supposed to be on the lake after nine, but this is a special situation. Just be sure to have it back in the dock by noon tomorrow. Can you do that?"

"I'll row them over," I said. "And I'll bring it back tonight."

"Great," Paul said. He looked at Maggie and Rodney.

"Agreed? Come on. I'll give you a ride to the dock. Try to be quiet crossing the lake. People are sleeping, and you know how sounds carry across the water."

We piled into Paul's jeep and rode to the dock. He walked us out to his boat. When we got there, he said to Maggie, "To be continued. Okay?"

She said okay, and Paul left. She'd been quiet and glum all the way in the jeep, and I guessed Paul was trying to patch things up, or at least make her feel better.

When we got into the boat, there was some confusion about who would do the rowing. Since I'd be rowing back, I figured Rodney would offer to row over. The flaw in my thinking was the prick factor, a major consideration when Rodney was involved. He said that since I had offered to "row them over," he assumed I would do all the rowing. He settled down next to Maggie, and I grabbed the oars, feeling like the victim of a clever lawyer.

Maybe Rodney had a romantic ride in mind, with me playing gondolier. If so, he was disappointed. As soon as we were under way, he and Maggie got into an argument. She started making all the points she'd made earlier, and he took Paul's side. They were getting loud, and I kept telling them to keep it down. Across the water I could hear a group of people on the beach. They sounded like College Joes making a long night of it. I didn't want to attract their attention. I kept saying "Shhh" to Rodney and Maggie, and they'd lower their voices for a few sentences, but then they'd get loud again.

Rodney said, "There's a chance Paul's right, which means we're exposing ourselves to a potential maniac every time we go up on those ridges. We're not going up there anymore."

"What about the aimah?" said Maggie. "You promised you'd help me find it."

"You're obsessed with that thing," Rodney said loudly. "That's all I ever hear from you. Aimah aimah aimah."

From the beach I heard a high shout of "Elmer!" and then some giggles. It took me a moment to figure out what had happened. Someone there heard Rodney and mistook his "aimah" for an "Elmer." Rodney and Maggie were silent. I didn't know if they'd seen this connection, and I was about to explain it to them, figuring maybe that would shut off the argument, but something interrupted me.

It was the orange buoy. I rowed right into it, and the *bong!* it made against the bow of the boat echoed all around the lake.

"Hey, keep it down out there," someone yelled from the beach, and there was more laughter.

"Way to go, Captain," Rodney said. He looked at the buoy.

I gritted my teeth. I didn't want Rodney thinking about that buoy, not for a second. But I had taken him right to it.

I rowed hard to get us away from there. Rodney stared at the buoy as we left it behind in the dark.

Eighteen

I was short of breath, but I kept climbing, moving at a steady pace. I was taking the same route up the mountain that I had taken before, with the river gorge on one side. The main difference was that this time I was all alone.

I had gotten up early to do this, my eyes popping open as if someone had shouted at me. But no one had. The cabin was empty. Maybe I had been dreaming. Maybe I was stirred up from our long discussion the night before. Whatever the reason, when I woke up I knew I had to do this.

I recognized the spot where we had rested, but I didn't rest. I kept going. I came to the place where I had watched Maggie and the others take off up the hill away from me. Last time I had gone all the way to the top from that point, and then I had run back down, chasing the deer. This time I cut out that middle step. I estimated where I had turned to go to the river gorge, and I turned and went that way again. I was moving across the mountain now, and the going was easier, so I broke into a medium run. Then I remembered the outcome of my last running experience up here and slowed right down to a walk.

But I couldn't find the place where I had almost met my maker. I found the gorge all right—places where the hill started to drop off—and I worked up and down in this area. But I couldn't find the hidden ledge with the sudden drop-off. It was tough work, with lots of hand climbing and bushes clawing at me. After about an hour I gave up.

I decided I had been lazy by cutting out that middle step. I needed to go all the way to the top and do it exactly the way I'd done it before. I resumed my climb and finally made it to the clearing at the top of the ridge.

There was a big flat rock in the clearing. I had rested on it when I was up here before, so I went to it and sat down. I would do everything the same way. The sun had risen just enough to touch it, and it felt good on my face. A wave of tiredness washed over me, and I lay back and shut my eyes. I had been pushing myself hard, and it felt good to lie there. I enjoyed the warmth of the sun on my skin and the weird dark colors it made on the insides of my eyelids. I spread my arms out, then my legs. I could feel the sun on the palms of my hands. The wind was whipping across the top of the ridge, and it sounded like a soft voice from another world. I just wanted to lie there forever.

I sat up and looked to the far edge of the clearing. I imagined the noises of the deer crashing through the woods, then the voices, then Maggie emerging and seeing me and yelling that I should steer the deer away from the lake. I stood up. I remembered the deer's surprise when he saw me. I could see him dart away, over the crest and down toward the next valley. I could hear the cheers from Maggie's group, then their groans when the deer reappeared and crossed the crest again, headed for the lake.

I shot straight down the mountain, doing it just like I'd done it before. I knew exactly when to turn and head for the river gorge. I knew it not because I remembered the place, but because I could see the deer again, in my mind, running right where he had run before, and I turned at the logical place to head him off. I tore through the woods, leaping over low bushes and rocks. I came upon a fallen log that guided me downhill a bit, and then I was on the wide path surrounded by brush.

I slowed down fast. The bushes rose high on each side of me, well over my head, forming a runway that guided me toward a hump of dirt. The sight of that hump made me stop completely. I stared at it—*glared* at it. Then I looked at the brush on both sides of me.

When Maggie had joined us on the beach and described what a motu was, she had said it was made of walls of brush that had been cut and stacked up. I wanted to see if these were those kinds of walls, or if the brush had just grown in a freaky way to form a natural path. I looked at the brush closely. It wasn't growing. It was stacked up. I felt the rough edges where it had been torn and sharper edges where it had been cut.

This was a motu.

As I pulled my hand back from the brush, I bumped a branch of it and several leaves came off and sprinkled on my arm and wrist. I looked at them and got a very strange feeling. What were leaves doing on these branches? How long did it take for leaves to fall off dead branches? A few days after they had been cut? A week, maybe two weeks? Certainly not a hundred years.

I walked along both walls of brush. They were

covered with dying leaves, making them a dull color, green fading to brown and gray. I shut my eyes and tried to remember what it had looked like a week earlier, when I'd run by it. I hadn't really examined it then. I'd only glimpsed it, sensed it. But my memory was of something green—bright green, freshly cut.

This wasn't just a motu. It was a motu that was about a week old.

This thought made me whirl around and search the woods with my eyes. I was scared. I held my breath to hear better. The only sound was the wind in the trees, which I could feel as well, blowing coldly out of the gorge and over that hump into my face.

I had to look at that ledge again. I had to. I took a few steps toward the hump. I felt myself getting top-heavy and dropped to my hands and knees. I crawled to the hump and looked over it. Ahead of me was the ledge, and beyond it the wind of the river gorge. And there were those pebbles on the ledge. Those slippery marbles of death.

I was suddenly suspicious about the pebbles. On my first trip up here, I had assumed they had dribbled down to the ledge from some nearby piece of granite that was eroding, but there was no such piece of granite in sight. On both sides of the ledge there was dirt and bushes, and the runway leading to it was all dirt. Up the hill I could see a few rocks, but they looked solid, and even if pieces of them did drop off, they would have stopped short of the ledge.

Someone had put the pebbles there.

Why? To kill a deer—to make it even harder for the animal to stop from falling. Had he killed one? Had *I* killed one? The deer I had chased the week before had escaped. Or so I had figured, anyway. Nate said he'd seen one just like it in the backyard of the cabin where he'd spent the night, just at the time when my deer would have gone by. But there could have been two bucks in the area that looked alike. Mine could have gone flying off the ledge just seconds before I almost did, and Nate could have seen a different one.

If I did kill a deer, where did he land? There was only one way to find out. I'd have to lean over the edge of the granite and look straight down.

I crawled over the hump and down the dirt path until it met the granite. I stopped. I was stuck. I reasoned with myself. If the ledge had been a diving platform, which was what it looked like, with a pool of water a safe distance below, I could easily have scooted out there on my belly, peeked over the edge, and then scooted back to safety. Couldn't I *pretend* it was a diving platform, in spite of the pebbles and the slight downward slope to it? Couldn't I?

I inched forward until my forearms were on the ledge. I stopped. Then I inched forward some more, until my arms and shoulders were on the ledge. I stopped again. Then I inched *backward, fast,* all the way to the hump, where I stopped and glared at the ledge. It was impossible. It was just impossible.

I got my bearings as well as I could, looking for landmarks across the river gorge and guessing just how far upriver I would have to walk to be in a position right under the ledge. I hoped I would be able to see where the ledge stuck out from down there. Farther upriver, I saw a column of smoke from a campfire. Rodney's camp. This was a great landmark, because from where I stood it was about as far upriver as the lake was downriver. All I had to do was go to the exact midpoint between Rodney's camp and the lake and I'd be right under the motu.

It was a quick trip back down to the lake—more of a controlled skid than a walk. I went along the lake and turned up the river trail, aiming for that column of smoke. My eyes roamed over the clifftop while I walked. About a quarter of a mile upriver, I stopped. I looked at the smoke. I looked back at the lake. I seemed to be in the right place. At the top of the cliff I thought I saw a piece of granite jutting out. I couldn't be sure, but it looked right.

I left the trail and headed straight for the base of the cliff. It wasn't far away, but it was rough going, over huge, rounded boulders that were tough to climb. When I reached the base of the cliff, I looked up. As far as I could tell, I was where I wanted to be. I looked all around the base of the cliff, a little nervous. Seeing dead stuff was always a shock. Even coming upon a dead squirrel threw me. To find a whole deer staring at me would be really strange. But then I realized the deer would be there only if *I* had made it fall from the cliff. If *he* had made one fall—whoever *he* was—he would have dragged it away. But there still might be some sign—some blood, some hair, a broken piece of antler.

If there was, I couldn't find it. I remembered it had rained one night during the week, and that might have washed away the evidence. Or maybe I was looking in the wrong place. Or maybe there was no evidence to find. Maybe that wasn't even a motu up there.

No. It had to be. The stacked brush. The pebbles. It had to be.

I went back to the river trail. I thought of going up to the camp, but I decided not to. I still wasn't satisfied with what I'd found, and I didn't want to tell

Maggie about it until I was.

As I walked back to the lake, I looked over my shoulder at the cliff a couple of times, wondering if I had been searching in the right place. At one point I looked from a spot on the trail that was hemmed in by boulders, and it reminded me of something Paul told me after his last tour. At first it didn't seem important. Then it did.

It was the story of the blond-haired little kid sitting on his father's shoulders, in a hemmed-in place on the trail, probably at this exact spot. The little kid's eyes had been higher than anyone else's in the tour group, and he had seen something nobody else had seen. And he had yelled, "Rudolph!"

Rudolph was a deer. Rudolph had a red nose. That wasn't important. What was important was something else about him.

Rudolph flew.

Nineteen

I was standing there looking at the cliff, picturing the deer soaring down, when I heard voices from up the river trail. They grew louder. One of them said, "It's at Slippery Slope, and I'm going right there as soon as we get back." That was Rodney, spreading the truth.

I heard Nigel say, "A treasure hunt. Such quaint customs you Americans have," and they rounded the bend and came into view. Lola was in front with the two of them, and the rest of the class followed.

"Ricky," Nigel said. "Hello-hello. We're on our way to examine the dam the early miners built—with some help from Miwok laborers, I might add. Care to join us?"

I said no, I had some stuff to do, and thanked him for asking. They passed by. I said hi to all of them, but I was really looking for Maggie. She was way at the back, which surprised me. She wasn't with Rodney, for one thing, and it wasn't like her to bring up the rear. She seemed almost depressed. I wondered if her cast and crutches were getting her down. But she smiled when she saw me and stopped.

"They think I'm crazy," she said.

"Listen," I said. "I figured out—"

"They think I'm nuts. I'm having one terrific idea after another, but when I try to share them with people, they just sneak glances at each other. They think I'm crazy. They think *he's* crazy too—whoever's up there. Lola's going to talk to Paul about it to see if he thinks she should move the camp somewhere else. She's afraid we'll all wake up one morning with our throats cut or something. She even talked about taking us back to Stanford to finish up the course in the classroom."

"Listen, Maggie. I found it again. It's a motu."

"What?"

"It's a motu. There's no doubt about it."

Her eyes widened.

"Something else," I said. "It's a *new* motu. It can't be much more than a week old."

She looked strangely happy. "You're on my side, aren't you?"

I hadn't really thought of it that way, but it was true. "Yeah. I guess I am. There's something else, too."

"There is?"

"It worked. He got his deer."

"Oh my God."

I told her everything—about the brush being newly cut, the pebbles, and my theory about the kid's "Rudolph." Her eyes darted swiftly back and forth as I talked. I couldn't believe how fast they moved.

"When did the little boy say 'Rudolph'?" she said. "When?"

Rodney's voice came shrilly from far down the river trail. "*Maggie? You coming?*"

Maggie ignored Rodney's shout. "When?"

"Last week."

"*Maggie!*" Rodney yelled.

Maggie glared down the trail and screamed her answer. "Go ahead! I'll catch up! Just shut up!" She looked back at me. "When last week? When exactly?"

"Monday," I said. "It happened on Paul's nature walk. He told me about it right after the walk."

She smiled and relaxed a little. "We chased the

deer on Saturday. If the little boy saw a deer fall off the cliff on Monday, someone else was chasing it."

"Right. Someone else."

"Hot damn," she said softly. I never said "hot damn" so I wasn't sure what she meant by it. But I think it was a happy noise. She hopped on her good foot to a small rock and sat down on it. "A new motu," she said. She looked up at me. "It's like everything else, Ricky. Everything we think is old is new. The snares. The quiver. Now the motu. And it's all so faithful to the Miwok way of life. I just can't believe it's a madman up there. It's got to be a Miwok."

I nodded. "Last night, when Paul said your theory had too many problems with it, I agreed with him. Now I agree with you. I think it's the real thing."

She looked at me a moment. Then she looked up at the cliff. "The question is . . . . Well, there are lots of questions, but one of them is how many are there? How many Miwoks? There's nothing to help us answer that. The hut Rodney and I found didn't have anything in it, apart from the quiver. I mean, it's not as if there were four toothbrushes in it or anything."

I laughed, which seemed to surprise her.

"I'll tell you one thing, though," she went on. "However many there are, one of them must be a lot younger than we were thinking. Twelve or thirteen, since he's going through the initiation ceremony. He's already completed the first part—the motu. Now he has to complete the aimah. If he can find the damn thing." This time she laughed. Then she grew serious again. "You know, the Miwoks really respect this river. They're always talking about it." She looked up the trail, upriver. "The aimah's along the river, Ricky, only way up there, on higher ground, farther than we've ever explored. Mark my words. It's up there somewhere."

I followed the course of the river up through the gorge with my eyes. I expected her to suggest we take off, right then and there, and try to find it. I looked at her cast. It was getting pretty beat up from all the walking around she had done already. I looked upriver again and pictured the young Miwok finding the aimah. And then what?

"What's he supposed to do with the aimah, Maggie? You said something about hair."

"All I know is what Chief O'Hara told me. He said, 'The boy gives it hair during the seventh darkness after the motu.'"

"'The seventh darkness.' That means the seventh night, right? If the motu was Monday—"

"—then the seventh darkness will be tomorrow night."

"Tomorrow night," I said. "Okay. We've got the

time, but what's the event? Does he put hair on the head of the aimah?"

"I don't know."

"Does he cut his own hair off and stick it on it?"

"I don't know. I thought of the hair that men have, since it's an initiation ceremony. Pubic hair."

"Ah." I had a dumb thought. I was afraid to ask it, but I had to. "Do Indians have any? I mean—"

Maggie laughed. "I wondered the same thing, briefly. They don't have as much facial hair as whites, but yes, they do have the other kind." She frowned. I've got to talk to Chief O'Hara again. I've got to see if I can get anything more out of him. And I want to see if he's ever heard a rumor about a group of Miwoks roaming the ridges."

"You know, I've got this feeling it's not a group."

"Really?"

"I think it's just one person. I have this feeling that he's all alone."

She thought about this. "Maybe. It's easier for one person to go unnoticed than a whole group. That would explain why nobody's seen them. But if there's just one—"

"—then how can he be young?"

"Yeah. Where are his parents? You'd think at least one of them would be alive."

I thought of something else. "That quiver you and

Rodney found."

"What about it?"

"It was pretty funky."

She laughed. "You said that last night."

"I mean, even for something made by hand out in the wild and all. Paul said it was crude. It looked like an inexperienced person made it."

"A young person."

"Yeah."

We sat in silence for a while, both of us trying to make more sense of it.

"What if . . ." said Maggie. But her voice trailed off.

"What?"

"What if he doesn't know where the aimah is? Suppose his parents died or something before they could tell him where it is."

"I don't know. What basis do you have for thinking that?"

"What if this happened a long time ago? I mean like over a hundred years ago."

"What if what happened?" I was confused.

"Suppose there was a Miwok boy who missed out on his initiation because no one told him where the aimah was."

"Over a hundred years ago?"

"Yeah."

I shrugged. "His problems are over. He's dead."

"But what if he stayed young because he didn't go through the initiation ceremony? What if he remained a boy?"

"For how long?"

"Forever."

I looked at her closely to see if she was kidding. She wasn't. "I'm not sure I'm still on your side, Maggie."

She laughed softly. Then she said, "There's a Miwok legend about that. The legend of the Eternal Youth."

"You mean the boy who was doomed to play soccer all his life?"

"Soccer?" She laughed. "You mean posko. You know the story?"

"Lola told me when I visited your camp."

"So you know he stayed young forever because he didn't complete his initiation. I wonder if that's what we're dealing with. An Eternal Youth roaming the ridges."

"I kind of doubt it."

She laughed. "I guess I do too. Oh, I have one more theory. It's silly, really, but it's worth sharing with you. You know how everyone around here always yells 'Elmer'?"

"Yeah. I've wondered about that myself. What's it got to do with this?"

"Remember what happened last night in the rowboat? Rodney said 'aimah,' and the guys on the beach thought he said 'Elmer' and yelled 'Elmer' at him. I was lying in my hut thinking about it, and I came up with the idea that 'Elmer' comes from 'aimah.' Yell 'aimah' real loudly and it sounds like 'Elmer.' Try it."

I started to, then said, "Another time. When I'm alone."

Maggie laughed. "Such a shy guy you are. Anyway, my theory is that this kid who's up there—just a regular kid, none of this Eternal Youth stuff—this Miwok boy who wants to become a man, has been yelling 'aimah' recently because he can't find it. Someone down here thought he was yelling 'Elmer,' and then 'Elmer' spread from there."

I laughed. "That's a great story. But there's a flaw in it."

"What?"

"They've been yelling 'Elmer' for a lot longer than you think. There's a photograph in the lodge that proves it." I told her about the photo of the fisherman, dated 1883, with the writing that said catching a fish like that made you want to shout "Elmer."

Maggie got a funny look on her face. I wondered

why, and then I knew. I knew it before she said it.

"My God, Ricky. What if the boy has been yelling it from the mountains all this time?" She looked up to the cliff and said, "What if he really is an Eternal Youth?"

Twenty

I walked with Maggie down to the lake trail. She was in a funny mood, sort of distant and preoccupied. I said a couple of things, and I had to repeat both of them before she heard me. She was about to go join the others down the trail, but there was one more thing on my mind. I said to her, "Maggie, you've been studying all this stuff about Indian initiation rites."

She said, "Yeah?"

"What's the initiation rite for us? For Americans?"

"We don't have one."

"What's a man then? What's the definition of a man?"

"What's *my* definition? Is that what you're asking?"

It wasn't, but I decided to go ahead and see what

she had to say. "Yeah."

"I would define a man in terms of behavior. A man behaves a certain way with people. He's kind. He's big. I mean big-hearted. Like a good father. He doesn't have to be a father, but he knows how to behave like one." Her eyes twinkled behind her glasses. "How does that sound?"

"Different."

"Well, that's me, I guess. See you, Ricky."

"See you." I watched her turn and head down the trail.

When I got back to the cabin, Nate was washing his car in the driveway. I was a little surprised to see him. I figured he'd be spending the day with Ally. He saw me out of the corner of his eye, but he pretended not to. He was just fooling around. I knew he'd seen me from the huge grin on his face. As I walked up to him he kept doing what he was doing—sponging the roof and grinning like a fiend.

"He shoots!" he suddenly said. He still hadn't looked at me.

"What?"

"He shoots!"

I couldn't figure out what he meant.

"He shoots!" He turned to me. "He *scores!*"

I laughed. "Well, what do you know?"

"A lot!" he said, as if I'd asked a real question. "A lot more than I knew twenty-four hours ago, anyway."

"Congratulations." I wasn't sure what to say. I'd never had this experience before.

"Thanks." He had a foolish, happy look on his face. I thought of Horace coming home after a wild night and plopping on Norman's porch.

"Tell me about it," I said.

Nate put on a shocked face. "Ricky. I'm surprised at you. This is a private matter. Very private indeed." He paused. "Where do you want me to start?"

I didn't have a chance to answer. He poured it all out. He talked me through every step, every phase, every garment, every square inch of an actual female human body. I was fascinated. This was as close as I'd ever gotten—a firsthand report, within hours of the event, by my best friend and a guaranteed nonliar besides.

"I'll tell you one thing," he said. "The whole idea of it being a conquest is ridiculous. It's not a conquest. It's not like climbing a mountain. Mountains don't suddenly relax. They don't suddenly flatten out."

I thought I got his meaning, but I wanted to be sure. "No metaphors, please. Give it to me straight. What do you mean?"

He picked up the hose and began to rinse off the roof and windows. "She's a *person*. She wanted the same thing I did. In the past, I figured I failed because I didn't know how to do it. I didn't pick the right route up the mountain. But that's not why."

"She's a doer. Is that what you're saying?"

"Hey," Nate said. "Let's not tarnish the occasion with Norman-talk." He fell silent and began washing the doors. He seemed to be done talking about it, but I didn't want him to be done. I struggled to think of a new way to get him to say more. "How was it different from how you thought it would be?" I asked.

He nodded thoughtfully. He was being a real scholar about it. "The funny thing is . . ." His voice trailed off.

"What?"

"I don't know how to put it, but it felt familiar."

"Hunh?"

"It felt like I'd done it before."

I laughed. "Maybe because you have. In your imagination. About seventeen billion times."

"But why would I imagine it right?"

He had me there. "Maybe you've imagined it all sorts of ways, some right and some wrong. The right ones made it feel familiar."

He smiled. "Your mind is so strange sometimes.

No. It didn't feel familiar because of my imagination. It felt like . . . part of the program. Like a computer program. Like it's in my nature to know how to do it."

"You're an animal, you mean."

He grinned. "Yeah."

"But Horace tried to screw dogs in their rib cage."

Nate laughed. "Sure. But eventually he worked his way around to the right place. It's instinct."

I suddenly remembered something. "I read once about a married couple who were so ignorant that they didn't do it. They didn't know how."

"Really?" Nate said. "That's pretty heavy. They must be weird cases. Isolated cases. Where'd you read that?"

"I don't know. *Junior Great Books?*"

He laughed. Then he was silent again. I *still* didn't want him to be done. "So," I said. "To sum up, was it fun?"

Nate screwed his face up in six different ways, really working on the question. Finally, he had an answer. "I've got to be honest, Ricky. At times it was . . . dazzling. But most of the time my mind was working so hard, and I was so busy watching myself, and so busy talking to myself, saying, 'You're doing it, Nate, you're doing it, you're doing it,' that . . . I don't know, *fun* just doesn't seem to be the right word for it."

"How about 'work'?"

He laughed.

"Was it fun for Ally?"

"Ha!" he said triumphantly. "I sent her to the moon."

I looked at him.

"I blasted her head off."

"Pretty good, hunh?"

Nate was looking at me closely. "Do you believe me about that? Do you believe that I sent her to the moon?"

I shrugged. "Sure."

"Don't."

"Hunh?"

"Don't believe me." He gave a little laugh. "It's so easy to lie. To bullshit. Look how well you know me, and I still could have fooled you." He shook his head sadly. "I didn't send her to the moon, Ricky. I didn't even send her to Ragtown. To be honest, to be really honest, I think I let her down."

"No. I don't believe it."

"I think I did."

"What makes you say that?"

"I just have this feeling."

"But you've got nothing to compare it with. Maybe it was great for her."

He gave me a little punch in the arm. "You kill me.

I score, and you try to cheer me up. What is this?"

"One more question, then. Do you feel like a man?"

He squinted and gave this some thought. "Yes," he finally said. "But I know it's dumb."

"Good."

"Good?"

"Yeah. Good that you know it's dumb. I don't want you lording this over me."

"Okay. I won't."

"You puff your chest out, you do anything like that, you're dead. Remember—I'm a wrestler."

"Okay. I'll be perfect."

"And if you ever *begin* to give me sexual advice—"

"—you'll remind me what a rotten time Ally had with me."

I frowned. I'd been kidding, but I felt like I'd somehow reminded him of this thing that was bothering him. "No I won't. I wasn't going to say that. You've got to stop thinking that."

He shrugged and reached for the hose.

I said, "Listen, I've got some news for you. Something totally different."

"What?"

"It's not about sex."

"Forget it then." He laughed. "Just kidding. Tell

me."

I told him all about the motu and my "Rudolph" theory. We hadn't talked about Horace's transformation into a quiver, so I told him about that, too. He'd heard the commotion Norman made at the dance, but he didn't know what it was about. He laughed, but then he got a serious look on his face.

"What is it?" I said.

"A strange thing just happened."

"What?"

"I felt sorry for Norman. I actually felt sorry for him, because of Horace." He shook his head. "Geez, I'll have to watch myself." His serious look was gone, and he was grinning again. I hadn't seen him this happy all summer.

Nate drove to Granite Springs after lunch to help his dad at the nursery. I hung out at the cabin. Ally called late in the afternoon, but Nate wasn't back yet. She asked me to tell him that she couldn't make it to the movie tonight, and that she'd see him tomorrow. I said okay. Before she hung up I heard some laughter in the background. It sounded like guys. I wondered if she was at a party.

Nate got back around dinnertime. His face fell a mile when I gave him the news about Ally. I didn't mention the guys laughing. I didn't want to make it worse.

We went to the outdoor movie together. It was *20,000 Leagues Under the Sea*—a kids' film, really, but I didn't feel too silly being there. After all, it was the only movie theater within thirty miles. Besides, I found something in it to add to our list of Fake Stuff in the Movies. It had to do with timing. There was this rousing song in the movie that everyone on the ship sang, and as soon as they were done—I mean the *instant* they were done—someone in the crow's nest yelled, "Ship ahoy," and all this excitement began. The timing was too neat. In real life the song would have been interrupted by the guy in the crow's nest, or there would have been this dead time after the song, with the sailors standing around bored and thinking "What now?" Real life was just messier.

I was the one who discovered this, and Nate understood what I was saying right away. He said yeah, it *was* phony. I think it took his mind off Ally. For a few seconds, anyway.

Twenty-one

Sunday was a beach day. But it wasn't your average beach day.

I strolled down there about noon. Nate had left a little ahead of me to pick up Ally at her cabin on the lake. They would join me later. When I got to the beach, I saw Nigel, Rodney, and two girls from the camp, and I walked over to them. The two girls were plugged into their Walkmans. One smiled at me. The one next to her was subtly grooving on her back with her eyes closed.

Nigel was staring at the lake. When he saw me, he brightened and said, "Ricky. Good man. Just in time to cheer up your poor brother. I'm afraid I've failed."

I sat down with them. "What's the problem?"

Nigel waited for Rodney to answer. When he

didn't, Nigel said, "He's misplaced his girlfriend. Can't seem to find her. He hasn't seen her since our little hike around the lake yesterday. A tragic state of affairs."

"I'm worried about her," Rodney said.

"He's worried about her," Nigel repeated. It was a funny thing to do, as if Rodney hadn't spoken.

"She said she had something to do," Rodney said.

"She said she had something to do," Nigel repeated. Rodney wasn't amused. Nigel must have sensed this because he stood up and said, "I believe I shall go for a little bathe now."

One of the girls giggled, but her eyes were closed. I couldn't tell if she was laughing at Nigel's expression or at something in her earphones. We watched Nigel trot down to the water. He stuck a toe in, yanked it out, and turned around and gave us a big wave right away, as if he knew we'd be watching.

"What did you two talk about yesterday?" Rodney said to me. He seemed tense.

"Maggie and me? We talked about what's up there." I looked to the ridge.

"I mean, did you come to any conclusions? Does she believe in it more than she did before?"

"We both think there's a young Miwok male living in the wild up there."

Rodney let a little spurt of air out his nose. He

shook his head slowly back and forth. This bugged me. I wanted to tell him about the motu. I wanted to tell him about the little kid's "Rudolph." But if he was going to be like that, I wouldn't tell him a thing.

Rodney looked down the beach. "Here comes Lola," he said.

She was with Paul Ling. I had never seen them together, and I wondered if they had just met. They were walking along the shore, and they paused when they reached Nigel, who hadn't gone for a "bathe" at all but was still standing at the edge of the water. The three of them talked for a while, and then Lola went on down the beach, toward camp. I was disappointed to see her go.

Nigel and Paul walked to where we were sitting. Nigel said, "We are spared, campers."

The two girls perked up and unplugged their earphones.

"Since no one's life has been directly threatened," Nigel went on, "Lola has decided that the camp will remain at Quiver River for the foreseeable future."

Rodney and the girls seemed relieved to hear this.

"Lola was being a little overprotective," Paul said. "I don't blame her. It's a big responsibility to be in charge of a group like yours. And I think Maggie may have exaggerated my concerns a little. Or maybe I'm to blame. Who knows? At any rate, Lola and I met. We talked. She feels better. So do I." He looked after her as she walked down the beach—appreciatively? Hungrily? It was hard to say. But I got the feeling he'd be making up reasons to drop in on the camp now.

"Sit down, Paul," I said.

He hesitated. "Just for a minute." He was wearing his Forest Service uniform, so it must have been a workday for him. He squatted in the sand, but he didn't look comfortable. He was always busy, always working, always talking. I got the impression he didn't know how to sit on a beach. He looked up at the sky as if he wanted to say something meteorological, but then he didn't.

Nigel was still standing. He said, "Come on, Rodney. I can't face that icy water alone. Let's swim out to the raft."

Rodney sighed, but he got up, took off his T-shirt, and went with Nigel down to the water. He had given me his T-shirt to hold. He was always doing that—treating me like an underling, a slave. I wadded it up and tossed it on the sand.

"It's still early in the season," Paul said. "The lake'll warm up a bit before long."

"Right," I said. I had asked Paul to sit down not just because I liked him, but also because I wanted to tell him about my talk with Maggie and our latest theories. But now that he was here beside me, I remembered how strictly scientific he was. I didn't want to deal with that right now. So I was quiet, and we sat and watched Nigel and Rodney ease into the water.

Then I saw someone I'd never seen on the beach before, at least not on a Sunday: Norman the Foreman. He walked by between us and the water. He had a hard look on his face.

"There goes an unhappy man," I said.

"You can say that again," Paul said. "The unhappiest man I know." This surprised me. I had meant my comment to apply to the way Norman looked right now. Of course I knew Norman was permanently unhappy. What surprised me was that Paul knew this about him.

"I've been working with him lately," I said. "It's awful. He's a nut case."

"He's not that bad."

"Yes he is. He's the worst."

"No. He's just unhappy. Give him a chance."

"I did. He blew it." I looked at Paul. "How well do you know him?"

Paul stretched his legs out. "He was a classmate of my brother's in school here, five years ahead of me." He smiled. "I'll always be grateful to Norman. My family was the only Asian family up here when I was a kid, and there were certain people who didn't like us."

"What do you mean? Racists?"

"Yeah. Racists. My brother had it worse than me, being older. He led the way. He was called 'Chink' more than I was. But every time someone did that, you know who stood up for him? Norman. My brother was small, and Norman was huge as a kid. He had a simple policy toward anyone who called my brother a Chink. He would smack them in the head, no questions asked." Paul laughed to himself. "Sometimes that's the best way to fight it, I guess."

"What made Norman do that? Why was he different?"

"I don't know. It's strange. There just seemed to be something inside him that couldn't stand it. My parents were crazy about him. But his luck took a bad turn in his last year of high school. His girlfriend got pregnant. In those days, when that happened you almost automatically married them, so he married her. They're still together, so it must have worked out tolerably, at least, but it sure messed Norman's life up. He managed to finish high school, but he had to put off college for years, so he could work full time, and then when he finally made it to college, it took him forever to get his degree. It changed his personality, that one thing, that one event. He's been sour ever since. And you know what? Sourness brings you more sourness. He's the unluckiest man I know. Nothing good ever happens to Norman."

I watched Norman reach the end of the beach beyond the lodge and then cross the dirt road to his cabin. My dad had an expression that he'd use at a time like this. "Everybody has a story." This was Norman's story—his life took a wrong turn and he never recovered.

Someone called out Paul's name from behind us. We turned around and saw another ranger approaching, walking fast and looking worried. Paul stood up and hurried to meet him. I watched them talk, but I couldn't hear what they were saying. I saw Nate beyond them. He was in the area where the volleyball net had been set up last week. He was alone, looking around. He headed toward me, frowning.

"You seen Ally?" he said when he reached me.

I said no. Nate grimaced and scanned the beach, squinting against the sun.

Paul came back and said, "I've got to go. There's been a bomb threat at the Lower River campground. We've got to check it out."

"A bomb threat?" Nate said.

"Yeah," said Paul. He started to say more, then shook his head. "I've got to go." He took off with the other ranger.

The girl near us had opened her eyes at Paul's return, but she must not have heard the news, because she just closed her eyes again and listened to her music.

Nate turned to me. I expected him to say, "Wow, a bomb threat!" Instead, he said, "I can't find Ally, Ricky. She's gone."

"She wasn't at the cabin?"

"No. No one's at the cabin. It's all shuttered up, like they've left for good. It's like she never existed. Did I imagine everything that happened?"

"She'll turn up. I'm sure she will."

"Maybe she found out I'm a liar. You think so?"

"I doubt it. How could she have found out?"

"Maybe I made a mistake. Maybe I said something only someone in high school would say. Or maybe someone told her the truth. You think Rodney could have told her?"

"No."

"He wouldn't do such a thing, hunh?"

"Oh, he'd do such a thing. But he couldn't have. He didn't know about the role you were playing. Besides, I don't think he knew her."

"Oh." Nate seemed even more despondent. "That

means she dumped me on my own merits. I must have been a disappointment." He gestured vaguely. He glanced at the two girls lying there and said more softly, "You know what I mean. This is her way of telling me."

"What makes you think you were a disappointment?"

"I don't know if I was or not. That's what's killing me."

"You were probably fine."

"I feel like a fool. Here I scored, and now I feel like a chump."

"Do you wish you hadn't scored?"

"Hell no," Nate said right away. He stood up. "I'm gonna go check the lodge. Hey, here comes Norman the Foreman. He's looking real good today. In top form."

Norman was walking along the beach again, returning from his cabin. He looked tired and unhappy. A heavy chain hung around his neck. He saw us and turned toward us. I wanted to tell Nate what Paul had told me about Norman, but I didn't have time. He was upon us too soon. Nate stuck around to see what he had to say.

"Someone broke into our toolshed," Norman said to me. He seemed to see me as a colleague. "They busted the lock. I'm gonna replace that dinky chain with one of mine. A big one. And look at this sucker." He dangled a huge padlock from his index finger. "Let 'em try and break this one, the bastards."

"Anything missing?" Nate asked.

Norman eyed him suspiciously, looking for sarcasm or mockery in the question. He said, "Bolt cutters."

Nate said, "Could bolt cutters cut through that padlock?"

Norman narrowed his eyes. I could see him imagining the same people breaking in again with the tool they had stolen in the previous break-in. It would be an endless cycle. Norman grunted and walked on.

The girl near me said, "Who's he?"

Nate said, "Oh, he's the local grammar school principal."

"Yeah, right," she said with a laugh.

Nate looked at me and shrugged. "I'm off," he said. "I'll be back." He headed for the lodge.

That left me alone for the first time with the two girls from the camp. One of them was still listening to her Walkman, but the one near me was up on her elbows looking at the lake. I was suddenly nervous and wished Rodney and Nigel would come back. But they were lying on the wooden raft.

"Your friend having romantic problems?" she asked.

I laughed. I was surprised she had heard us talking about this. "Yeah," I said.

"That kind of thing seems to be going around."

I looked at her. "You mean Rodney and Maggie?"

"Oh, them too."

I spent some time thinking about this. "Oh, them too" meant she hadn't been referring to them, so she must have meant someone else. Herself? Why would she tell me she was having romantic problems? To let me know she was available? I chewed over this possibility and took another look at her. She was prettier than the last time I looked. Did she know I was a high school student? Would that matter? I looked at her again. She had put her Walkman back on and was lying down with her eyes closed.

Something told me I had been a little slow there.

When Nate came back from the lodge, he looked as miserable as Norman the Foreman.

"I got an update," he said.

"Yeah?"

"Bad news. Jim saw her." This was the dining-room busboy we knew from Ragtown.

"Yeah?"

"She was at the front desk with the two guys we

played volleyball with."

"Yeah?"

"They were asking where they could rent some scuba equipment."

"So what?"

Nate looked from me to the girls, then said in a whisper, "I'm afraid they're going to explore the lake. I'm afraid she might have blabbed."

"Uh-oh."

"Thank God I didn't tell her exactly where it is. All I told her was that it's in the lake. Geez, I feel sick about it."

I was worried too. But Nate was so depressed I didn't want him to see it. "Maybe there's a harmless explanation, Nate. Maybe they want to scuba dive just for the fun of it. Somewhere up the highway. I've seen scuba divers at Lake McBride. But even if she did blab and they dive here, it's a big lake. They won't find it."

"Man, I'd never forgive myself if I ruined it. I don't trust those guys."

"Don't worry about it. Really. Forget it."

He sighed. "I don't trust her, either. Geez, I barely know her." He stared morosely out at the lake.

Twenty-two

After dinner Nate put in a lot of time on the phone, calling people with the same last name as Ally in Oakland, where her parents lived, in case she had gone back there. Unfortunately, her last name was Johnson, and there were a lot of them. Nate asked for a bunch of numbers from Oakland information, but they'd give him just a few at a time. He'd try these, strike out, then call information again for more. His nervousness filled the cabin up, and I had to get out of there.

I took a walk through the campground. Sunday was a getaway day for a lot of the campers. Arrival day too, for their replacements. A lot of them were still setting up, and I watched them as I strolled by. When I got back to the cabin, Nate had taken off and left a note behind. He hadn't reached Ally in Oakland, so he was driving up the highway in hopes of finding her at the cabin where some friends of hers were staying, near the pass, thirty miles away. This was a desperate move. I didn't think he even knew for sure where this cabin was. His note asked if I could stick around the cabin in case Ally called. I didn't mind. Nobody called. Nate was still out when I went to bed. I imagined him driving endlessly up and down the highway.

It was a wild night. I woke up several times, tossed around by the kind of dreams I'd had when I was sick with a fever—lots of voices, the same things happening over and over, and confusion about whether I was awake or not. At one point I heard sirens in the distance—a rare sound up here that usually meant a forest fire. I wondered if there had really been a bomb at that campground, and if it had gone off. Then I thought of Nate on the highway, and I jumped out of bed and went to his room.

He was in there, alone, sound asleep in his clothes on top of the bed. He hadn't even taken his jean jacket off. I stood there looking at him a moment before I went back to bed. I fell asleep and woke up to the sound of sirens again, only they were closer. I went downstairs. By the time I got out to the front porch, the sirens had stopped, but I heard faint voices in the distance, way down by the lake. It was barely light.

I got dressed and went back outside. I couldn't hear the voices anymore, but I took off for where I thought they had come from. The campground was quiet. It was cool and there was a faint mist in the air. When I rounded the bend that brought me to the picnic area, I took a look through the trees to see if anyone was down at the beach. I saw something I didn't expect to see.

All the water was gone.

I tore through the picnic grounds and ran across the sand to the edge of the lake— or what had been the lake. Now it was just a shallow bowl coated with a layer of dark mud. Tree stumps stuck up through the goo. Boats that had been floating at anchor sat plopped in the mire. The boats that were tied to docks were still tied up, but they didn't drift— they hung. Some had broken their ropes and had crashed to the mud below.

Way down at the end of the beach, just beyond the lodge, a group of people and trucks were gathered on the dirt road. I couldn't see what they were doing. They seemed congested somehow, packed together. I looked around for someone nearby to talk to, to verify what I was seeing, to tell me I wasn't crazy. I ran down the beach a ways, feeling a little panicked. I stopped and stared out at the lake bed again.

As I stood there trying to figure out what could have made this happen, it occurred to me that among the boats and junk lying in the mud was a waterproof metal box with a document in it good for two thousand bucks. That box was my responsibility. I spotted the orange buoy lying in the middle of the lake bed, but I couldn't see the box. I took off for the buoy and my feet immediately flew out from under me, landing me so hard in the mud that it felt like someone had thrown me down. I stood up and almost fell right down again. It was the slipperiest stuff I had ever been on. Running was out of the question. I tried walking carefully, but I got slammed down again. I finally resorted to taking mincing little baby steps.

As I walked, I kept expecting to see hordes of people coming out to pounce on the treasure. I suddenly thought of Ally and the two guys she had been with. I had a wild notion that they were somehow behind all this. I kept my eyes peeled for the box and finally saw it, next to the buoy. I couldn't tell if it had been opened or not. I wanted to run but all I could do was mince along.

I finally reached the box. It was intact, still welded shut. There were no footprints around it. I bent down and reached for it, but then I caught myself. I stood back up, suddenly aware of a tricky question I had to answer: Should I confiscate the box and find a new hiding place, or should I simply let things be?

I thought about it. What was the role of the hider of the treasure? To hide it and write clues until someone found it. Preferably they would find it by interpreting the clues, but sometimes they found it by accident. Now that some calamity had emptied the lake and exposed the box, should I intervene and pick it up, or should I let events unfold on their own? It was tough to know. I felt like I needed someone to help me. Someone like God, or my parents, or Nate.

But not Rodney. Not Rodney. Of all the people in the world, I didn't want that to be Rodney coming toward me from the far side of the lake bed—or rather, not coming toward me but falling in the mud. From the way he swore and looked mad as he got up, I knew: It was Rodney.

I looked at the box. I looked at Rodney. I looked at myself: I looked inward and forced myself to be honest. I had been leaning toward a decision not to touch the box. I should go ahead with that decision even though Rodney was closing in on me and the treasure. I would let things be. I would let it happen as it was destined to happen.

I watched Rodney slip along. He stopped and peered at me when he was about halfway to me. "Ricky," he yelled. "Is that you? What happened?"

I didn't say anything. What could I say?

"Cheez, can you believe this? Did the dam break?" He peered across the lake bed in the direction of the dam. "I can't see it from here."

I didn't speak. I could have said I didn't know what happened, but I didn't want to. I had this strange feeling that it wasn't right to speak.

"This is incredible," Rodney said as he got closer. "What a mess. What a complete mess. People are going to freak out when they see this."

This was true, I thought. The box was behind me. He hadn't seen it yet.

When he reached me, he said, "I woke up and checked Maggie's hut. She's still not back. You seen her?"

I shook my head.

Rodney scanned the lake bed. Something caught his attention, but it wasn't the box. "Hey, what's this stuff?" He walked some distance away and bent down.

I joined him. He was hunched over a pile of burned wood. There were footprints all around it. They weren't mine and they weren't Rodney's. He picked up a piece of the wood. "Damn!" he yelled, dropping it. "It's still hot." He brushed his hand on his pants and licked his fingers.

I bent down to the burned wood. It was black, but below it was ash, as if quite a fire had burned.

"This makes no sense," Rodney said. "Who came out here and built a fire in this muck?" He looked around the lake as if for an answer. "And who's that?"

I looked up. Someone had emerged from the cluster of people on the dirt road and was coming toward us. It was Norman the Foreman. He walked with a determined stride. I expected him to fall down, but he didn't.

"Ricky," Norman yelled. "Is that you? What the hell's going on?"

Everyone seemed to think I had the answer to this question.

"Who's that with you?" Norman yelled.

Rodney looked at me, then at Norman. "I'm Rodney," he yelled. "Ricky's brother." He looked back at me and smacked me on the arm. "Why aren't you talking? Snap out of it."

"What's going on?" Norman shouted.

"Who knows?" yelled Rodney. "People are gonna freak." This seemed to be the most interesting aspect of the situation to him. I looked around the lake bed. People were coming out of cabins, out of tents, out of the lodge. They were coming out and they were freaking.

"Amazing!" Norman said when he got close. He'd made it all the way without falling. "Forty-six years I've lived here, and I've never seen anything like this. Where'd the water go?" He looked all around. "Hey, what's this?"

His eyes were on the box. Rodney and I watched him walk over, pick it up, and shake it. He stared at it in his hands. Then he took a step toward the orange buoy, bent down to it, and began to bang the box against the buoy, trying to crack it open. He banged it about a dozen times. On the last couple of swings he brought the box high over his head for a real big bang.

"Damn. That's quite a welding job." Norman stared at the box some more. He tugged at it and frowned at the wire holding it to the buoy line. He took a knife from his pocket, and with a little pair of cutters on it he snipped the wire. He grunted with satisfaction, then said, "I'm gonna take a sledgehammer to this sucker." We watched him wander off across the lake bed, toward his cabin, with the box tucked under one arm like a football.

I tried to figure out what I felt as I watched Norman go. I wasn't upset. I didn't want to stop him or get the box from him. I was mainly just curious about how things were turning out. So that's how it ends, I thought. So that's how it was meant to be.

"Hey, there was another fire over here," Rodney said. He had walked around a big raised area in the mud, which was about waist high. The raised area was covered with mud, so it was hard to see what it was.

Rodney said, "Was there a party out here? I don't get it. What happened?"

The answer came from high on the mountain-top, on the ridge where I had chased the deer. It came in the form of a clear, piercing shout that sounded like "Elmer."

"Elmer to you too, pal," Rodney muttered, throwing a glance at the mountain. He thought it was just some regular tourist yelling it.

"Aimah!" I shouted at the mountain. "Aimah!"

Rodney said, "What in the hell are you doing?"

I ran around the rock, slipping and falling all the way, trying to see it—to *see* it. But I couldn't, not the way I wanted to. I hauled myself up on top of the rock and looked down. I *thought* I could see it, but I wasn't sure. I took off for the mountaintop, ignoring Rodney and his lame shouts at me.

I was exhausted from slipping by the time I reached the shore, but it felt so good to be on firm land that I was able to keep going. I crossed the lake trail and shot up the mountain. Halfway up I had to rest, I just had to. But I didn't turn around. I forced myself not to. After a minute I took off again, scrambling, using my hands now, zigzagging where I had to but trying to go up as straight and as fast as I could.

When I got to the top of the ridge, I thought my chest would burst. I turned around to see the lake, but the woods were too thick. I found a tree the right size and began to climb it. I moved fast, hand over hand, not stopping until I knew I would be able to see.

And then I did. I looked, and I laughed. Stretched out in the middle of the lake bed was the form of a large human body. It was rounded and featureless, like dough cut from a cookie cutter. Its legs were spread slightly apart, and its arms were stretched wide to each side. The head looked perfectly smooth and round.

In three crucial places, fires had been built: one at each armpit of the figure and one in its crotch. The fire wasn't as important as the charred black wood left behind by the fire, and what it looked like from this height.

The aimah was complete. Our young Indian brave had endowed it with the hair of a man.

Twenty-three

I climbed down the tree and skidded all the way back down the mountain. When I reached the lake trail, the empty bowl of the lake was crowded with people, wandering around as if they expected to find the explanation for what had happened out there in the mud. I could see the whole lake bed before me, with all the people in my field of vision, and every ten seconds or so someone's feet would go out from under them and they would hit the mud.

I wanted to find the explanation too, but I knew it wasn't out there. I turned up the trail to circle around the back side of the lake. But at the footbridge my way was blocked by a hand-printed sign strung across it. It read, "DANGER—BOMB THREAT— TRAIL CLOSED." I looked beyond the bridge to where the trail wound around the lake. I didn't see any activity—no bomb crews, no policemen, no one.

"Nah," I said. "I don't believe it." I reached out to tear down the sign, but then I pulled my hand back and crawled under it instead, leaving it there. I decided I shouldn't make the decision for anyone else and expose them to danger.

I stopped in the middle of the bridge. When I looked up into the mountains, I saw the river the way it had flowed through the gorge for centuries and centuries. "An old river," Paul had called it. When I looked downriver, I saw something new— new to me, anyway. But in a bigger sense, it, too, was old. It was the way the river had flowed for almost all of its life, before the white men came and built the dam that flooded the meadow.

With my eyes I followed the river along the edge of the muddy bowl all the way to the dam. There was the explanation. I could see the spillway beside the dam, with its adjustable iron gate that could be raised or lowered to control the level of the lake. Someone had "adjusted" it. It was wide open. The river poured through it as if it was chasing all the lake water that had drained through it the night before.

I ran long and hard all the way to the dam. I came

to a stop at the spillway and stared at the water. I thought I heard someone call my name, but when I looked around I couldn't see anyone. Then I thought I heard it again. I went back down the trail to get away from the noise of the water, and then I heard it clearly.

"Ricky! Get away from there."

It was Maggie's voice. I yelled to the wooded hillside, "Where are you?"

"Get away. They'll think you did it."

I still couldn't see her. "Where *are* you?"

She jumped into view on top of a big boulder, way up there. "Get your ass up here!" she screamed. Then she disappeared again behind it. I took off up the hill, keeping my eyes on that boulder as I worked my way up. I reached the downhill side of the boulder, worked my way around it, and found Maggie sitting cross-legged on top of it.

"Sit down," she said. "It's nice here."

"Nice?" I said. "Nice? It's a crazy day, God knows what you've done, and you say it's nice?"

"Sit. We don't want to be seen. Look." As I sat down, I looked to where she was pointing, at the trail on the other side of the dam. A big group of people were coming toward the dam—forest rangers, policemen, and highway patrolmen. "My sign held them up just long enough," she said. "I knew they would come to close the gate when they got word the river was rising. I knew it. But I slowed them down." She laughed devilishly. "Was my sign still up the way you came? On the bridge?"

"*You* made that? Geez, Maggie. What have you gotten yourself into here? There was a bomb threat yesterday on the campground on the lower river. You didn't do that too, did you?"

"Guilty," she said.

"I can't believe you."

"You didn't want all those tourists being flooded out of their campsites, did you? I thought it was very considerate of me to have them evacuated. I even went down there in the middle of the night, before I did my number on the spillway gate, to make sure there weren't any campers on the river who hadn't gotten the word. I didn't see any. But all that hiking finally wore out my cast." She pointed at her ankle. In place of the cast was a splint she had made out of sticks and one of her pants legs. "It's been a busy night," she said.

I looked down at the aimah, which stood out clearly from here. "Did you see him?"

"No. But I saw his work." She stared at the aimah. "I climbed up here in the dark and waited. I saw the fires—saw them spring to life as he lit them. It was all I could do to sit still. I wanted to shout to him. I wanted to yell every Miwok word I knew that would make any sense to him—'hello,' 'welcome,' 'good-bye.' I wanted to run down there and see him more than anything. But I stayed here. I made myself stay here. By the time it was light, he was gone."

Maggie looked sad. She also looked tired. I noticed a pair of bolt cutters on the rock next to her. All I could do was shake my head and laugh.

Maggie saw where I was looking. "I needed them to cut the big chain locking the gate valve."

"I'll take them back to the shed when I go to work."

"No, Ricky. That would make you an accessory after the fact. Actually, I shouldn't even be talking to you. I shouldn't have called out to you. That was stupid of me."

"I would have guessed it was you anyway."

"Do you think anyone else'll guess?"

I thought about this. "Maybe Rodney."

"Yeah. But he'll be so freaked out that he won't even want to bring it up." She laughed.

"How did you know the aimah was under the lake?"

She smiled. "Yesterday, after we talked, I joined the others at the dam. I got there just in time for the guy to show us how the gate valve works." She laughed again. "Then Lola sat us down and told us about the Quiver River Rebellion. I'd heard the story a million times. All these Miwoks who had been working peacefully to help build the dam suddenly changed their minds and tried to tear it apart. The whites resisted, the Miwoks fought back, and by the time they were done, two Miwoks were dead. The rest of the Miwoks took off and never came back. Lola told us no one had ever figured out what made the Miwoks go crazy like that. Well, that was on my mind, really brewing, when I left the others and went to the lodge. I wanted to see that photograph you told me about, with 'Elmer' written on it." She smiled. "Know what I saw?"

"What?"

"The aimah."

"What do you mean?"

"It's in one of the pictures. There's a whole bunch of pictures hanging in there—"

"I know."

"And some of them are of the meadow before it was flooded."

"I know that too. I've seen them."

"Then you've seen the aimah. It's in one of those pictures, plain as day. It doesn't look like a person, the way it does from here, because it's viewed from ground level, but it's this big flat rock all by itself out in the middle of the meadow. I saw that picture, and

I thought of the Quiver River Rebellion, and everything came together. All the other pieces fit too—how old 'Elmer' is, how the Miwoks never come to the lake, even to this day. In fact, they won't even say 'Quiver Lake.' They call the lake 'Quiver River,' as if they're denying it's a lake, or saying that a lake has no right to be here. When I figured out where the aimah was, I knew what I had to do. I didn't hesitate for a minute."

I sat there for a minute, putting the pieces together the way she had done. "You know, yesterday we were sort of half right."

"What do you mean?" she said.

"We knew he needed the aimah. We were right about that. But we were wrong in thinking he didn't know where it was. He knew. He just couldn't get to it."

"Yeah," said Maggie. "He couldn't complete the aimah. You can't start a fire under water."

"Why didn't Chief O'Hara just tell you all this?"

"I don't think he knew. He knew an aimah once existed, but that's all. The rest of it was tradition with roots that he probably didn't understand—the jinx on the lake, calling the lake Quiver River, all that." She frowned and was quiet for a long time. "I have this strange feeling, Ricky. I almost feel like I was chosen to help this Indian boy. And I feel like you were too, because I couldn't have done it without you. I feel like we were destined to bring an end to his boyhood."

I looked out at the lake bed, full of people moving around in confusion and wonder.

Maggie said, "Just think. If we hadn't come along, this boy would have stayed at the threshold of adulthood forever."

I said, "I can't imagine anything more horrible."

"I figure he'll go on to live a normal life now. I hope so anyway. And I hope he's happy. Happy to be a man."

I looked high up to the mountaintop. "He is. I know he is."